We Touched Heaven

Heaven

CLAUDIA WATTS EDGE

WE TOUCHED HEAVEN

An International Collection of Experiences that Reached Beyond the Veil

Copyright 2021 by Claudia Watts Edge

ISBN # 978-0-999-46352-9

Library of Congress # 2021905647

Retail, Wholesale, Bookstores, Libraries, Academic:

eStore www.amazon.com/dp/999-46352-9

Printed by Kindle Direct Publishing, An Amazon.com Company

In cooperation with LilyBud Publishing

Cover Image by Dmitry Molchanov, release Dreamstime, standard license.

Cover Design by Claudia Watts Edge

CLAUDIA WATTS EDGE

Author of the award-winning series GIFTS FROM THE EDGE

WE TOUCHED HEAVEN

An International Collection of Experiences that Reached Beyond the Veil

Foreword by Reverend Bill McDonald

Featuring: Mila Andelman, Enos Anderson, Jennifer Ann, PMH Atwater, Elizabeth Boisson, Sandra Champlain, Caroline Chang, Rebecca Austill-Clausen, Chelsea Clayton, Jesse Clayton, Chase Skylar DeMayo, Frank D'Silva, Penny Freeman, Becki Hawkins, Ingrid Honkala, Jenny Kennedy, Deb Kosmer, Genny Krackau, Teresa L, Brownell Landrum, Ritu Lebouef, Barbara Mango, Rev. Bill McDonald, Steve Marr, Sue Pighini, Sharlan Oskins, Susan Redwine, Ken Root, Lilia Samoilo, Emilie Spear, Kathleen Sterling, Alan Stevenson, Fiona Sutton, Janet Tarantino, Marion Terry, Chelsea Tolman, Gregg Untenberger, Ann Lotte Valentin, Larry Vorwerk, Jeff Watts, Ellen Whealton, Lee Witting, Tony Woody.....

THE BEST

Teachers

ARE THOSE WHO SHOW YOU WHERE TO

look

BUT DON'T TELL YOU WHAT TO

see

Alexandra K Trenfor

FOREWORD

By Rev. Bill McDonald Jr.

There are times in our lives when inspiration is just what the doctor ordered; and as a "spiritual doctor of the soul" myself, I recommend reading this book. It not only inspires the reader to go deeper within but adds the fuel and energy to totally refocus on loving, healing and believing in the greater purpose of it all. Author and our guide on this group spiritual journey, Claudia Watts Edge, provides entertainment, pieces of enlightenment, wisdom, heartfelt healing and loving energy, sharing and honoring the individual stories within these sacred pages.

This is a collective of LOVE and HOPE which feeds our needs for FAITH and TRUST in the Divine purpose of it all. Some stories will take us into the physically painful world and hard circumstances that others have faced. Others will move us emotionally to change the way we see our own life situations. Every person's true-life experience is special and conveys its own meanings. A few will deepen our faith about the afterlife. Most will leave you with little choice but to believe that there was a greater power and purpose at play in all that happened.

These stores, although they seem so different, belong with each other like family members. Each so different, yet all retaining that Divine grace of love and wonder. These are truly consciousness

i

expanding personal glimpses into who we all are as fellow human beings. We begin to realize, that maybe we are ALL just one family, sharing this life experience together. There is a connective energy, some may call it love, that binds us with our Divine source. These life stories tie us together with some universal truths and with tales that seem to be truly miracles.

There are no coincidences, or accidents, in our lives. Everything in this creation is on purpose. There is no randomness in how things unfold, even if we cannot determine the origins, or the rhyme, or reason, to why events happen in our lives. Our lives have a much greater purpose than just existing to breed and breathe. We all are seeking in our own way, a pathway back to the LIGHT. How we choose to follow our own "yellow brick road" is determined by our own free will. I do believe that we create our own futures. We may interpret what happens to us by all our choices, thoughts, and actions, and for those who believe – KARMA. It matters not if you hold onto that belief system or not, one has to trust that there are reasons for all that happens.

You the reader of this book (truly a seeker) are about to be changed in some subtle and not so obvious ways. Reading these stories is a true journey of heart and spirit. There is much energy in these fragments from others' lives. In the process you will find yourself transported to other realities and perhaps other dimensions with infinite possibilities. This is all about surrendering your limited perceptions and opening your heart and soul to a fuller awareness of the many facets of the Divine spiritual nature that surrounds us. Miracles are real! Love is real! GOD is REAL!

Things happen to us throughout our lives that appear to be horrible, ugly, or even painful at the time. However, the secret, that is not so secret, is that everything that happens to us is all about our own spiritual evolution. Reading these personal experiences of others, you will see how events lead the experiencers to discover greater truths about who they were and what their lives are truly about.

Getting stuck by lightning, or having your heart stopped several times, or hearing those inner voices that lead you to a safer place, or guide your life, are not as uncommon as one would think. These stories presented here are just a tip of the iceberg of a spiritual vastness of lovingness and joy that surrounds us all every day and in every moment. Read and embrace these stories and savor them as if they were your own personal experience. They did not happen just for those who shared their experiences but for the greater of mankind, it is for us all! The Divine is crying out to be heard and seen by all, not just the chosen few. They say that seeing is believing but I say that "Believing is seeing!" When you become childlike and are open to the LIGHT you will see!

Once you have opened this book and read the stories you will never be the same again. And that is a good thing! Enjoy the voyage!

Reverend Bill McDonald Jr

Author, ("*Alchemy of a Warrior's Heart*", "*Warrior a Spiritual Odyssey*", "*I Still Remember Tomorrow*") Award-Winning Poet, International Inspirational Speaker, Vietnam War Veteran (*The Distinguished Flying Cross, The Bronze Star, The Purple Heart, 14 Air Medals*) Documentary Film Consultant, Artist,

3-Time Near-Death Experiencer, Founder of *The Spiritual Warrior Ministries*, Yoga Meditation Teacher.

AUTHOR'S NOTE

Dearest Reader,

Contained within these pages are personal accounts of life-changing events from many wonderful people from all walks of life, and from all parts the globe. This celebrated collection comes from decorated military veterans, medical doctors, nurses, healers, hospice workers, therapists, psychologists, hypnotherapists, authors, teachers, musicians, a NASA scientist, marine biologist, chaplin, minister, funeral director, real estate agent, screen play writer, a newspaper columnist, and several PhDs and researchers who have spent a lifetime studying the phenomenon of the Spirit and the Light.

The following accounts also represent different belief systems, from atheists to practicing Hindus, with thought-provoking answers tied to suicide, dementia, HIV, battlefield death and traumas, and even the devastating loss of a child through miscarriage or on Mount Everest. It offers a variety of healing techniques and therapy resources for illness and disabilities through music, and a new technique called Brainspotting that can heal a previous-life trauma.

Through acts of synchronicity and circumstance, they were brought together in one place—your hands, dear reader. In my many years as a seeker, I have learned that there are no accidents, and the fact that you are holding this book right now is an indication that you too are ready to expand your awareness of the life beyond this one.

I have purposefully included accounts of afterlife communication through dreams and Near-Death Experiences (NDEs), and through the wonders of life-changing experiences Spiritually Transformative Experiences (STEs) while hunting, behind the wheel of a car, on the toilet, or simply by taking a walk.

The old saying of when you are ready, the teacher will appear, seems to be more than a philosophy as you will discover in the following stories. You will find that it is possible to have a conscious experience with the light without having to die. The universe opened up before them, offering answers and unwavering love and protection, thus changing their perspective and entire belief systems, all because they were simply open to that very possibility.

Hold on to the stories from the contributors that resonate with you, as they can act as a guide and a road map to assist you on your personal journey.

These stories are gifts, and were collected especially for you dear reader, and they are offered here with a full and open heart.

Most Sincerely,

Claudia Watts Edge

Author of

GIFTS FROM THE EDGE Stories of the Other Side

GIFTS FROM THE EDGE Volume II Lessons from the Other Side

WE TOUCHED HEAVEN

> **"**
>
> When you stand and share your story in an empowering way, your story will heal you and your story will heal somebody else.
>
> - Iyanla Vanzant'

I want to Thank the following Beautiful Souls who Willingly Shared their Personal Wonders with me,
and Now with the World.

Mila Andelman—Vancouver, BC Canada

Enos Anderson JP, Ct, Hyp, PLR Jamaica

Jennifer Ann New Jersey

PMH Atwater LHD—Charlottesville, VA

Elizabeth Boisson—Phoenix/Scottsdale, AZ

Sandra Champlain—Byfield, MA

Caroline Chang—Tobyhanna, PA

Rebecca Austill—Clausen, Downingtown, PA

Chelsea Rose Clayton—West Jordan, UT

Jesse Warren Clayton—Salt Lake City, UT

Chase Skylar DeMayo—Orlando, FL

Frank D'Silva—Perth, Australia

Penny Freeman—Wallsend, New South Wales, Australia

Becki Hawkins—OK

Ingrid Honkala PhD—Columbia/USA

Deb Kosmer—Oshkosh Wisconsin

Genny Krackau—San Antonio, TX

Brownell Landrum—CO

Jenny Kennedy—Mount Maunganui, New Zealand

Teresa L—AZ

Ritu Lebouef—TX/India

Barbara Mango PhD—Northeast United States

Steve Marr—Cape Town, South Africa

Reverend Bill McDonald Jr.—CA

Sharlan Oskins—West Jordan, UT

Sue Pighini— Frederickburg, VA

Susan Redwine—Franklin, NC

Ken Root—Pacific Northwest USA

Lilia Samoilo— PA

Emilie Spear—Denver, CO

Kathleen Sterling—Seattle, WA

Alan Stevenson—Ontario, Canada

Fiona Sutton—Midlands, UK

Janet Tarantino—Windsor, CO

Marion Terry—Lake Wales, FL

Chelsea Tolman—Salt Lake City, UT

Gregg Untenburger M.Ed.LPC.—Georgetown, TX

Dr Lotte Valentin N.MD—Phoenix, AZ

Larry Vorwerk—Northfield, MN

Jeffrey Watts—Salt Lake City, UT

Ellen Whealton—Carlsbad, CA

Rev. Dr. Lee Witting—Castine, ME

Tony Woody US Navy Chief Petty Officer —Exeter, NH

Contents

"Doubt everything,
but always keep an open mind,
an open mind has the potential
to make great discoveries."

Words spoken to Ingrid Honkala PhD,

from the BEINGS OF LIGHT

Chapter One

EXTRAORDINARY NEAR-DEATH EXPERIENCES

Sue Pighini	DIVINE DIALOGUES
Emilie Spear	POOL OF PEACE
Susan Redwine	THE DIVINE REMEMBRENCE AND INFORMATION IS NOT DISCRIBABLE (but I will try)

DIVINE DIALOGUES

Adoration for YOU from the Angelic Realm

By Sue Pighini

You are Extraordinary! Expect the Extraordinary in YOUR life! I certainly didn't know what that meant in 1972 when I was struck by lightning in the Arizona mountains. My life was saved by a voice, which I call angelic, that told me to move my legs back and forth, back and forth, to save my heart from the "fire" of the lightning coursing through my body. I was having a near-death experience. I had no idea what that meant either. I had never heard of near-death before. I just knew I had touched the "other side." This exceptional event put me on a path of searching for the meaning of my life. Why was I still alive? Why was I here? Just like you I wanted to know if heaven was real, if angels were real. Little did I know that this experience was just the beginning of having my questions answered.

Then, in 2016, after launching my second book, "Expect the Extraordinary", I was on a radio interview and saw a ball of white lightning come across the field in front of me and it entered my forehead. What was that? Whatever it was I was on the floor having trouble breathing. I found my cell phone next to me and speed dialed my husband. With his medical background, he knew immediately that I was having a brain aneurysm. It was nine days in intensive care before the neurosurgeon could find the bleed in a very obscure location behind my right ear. As I was going into the third exploratory surgery, I was just so tired. I just wanted to rest – forever. Too much, too overwhelming. As I was getting prepped for the angiogram procedure, there appeared 12 small, childlike angelic beings around the surgical table. And, one very large being in white to my right over my shoulder. "We have you. You are safe. You are loved." With a smile on his face. The love was palpable and electric. I was having my second near-death experience.

It was now 2019 and I had just found out that I had skin cancer for the second time on my nose, and it had to be removed immediately. (I had put it off, being human and all.) This was a two-part surgery, three weeks apart. Part one was a success as the plastic surgeon removed the basal cell cancer growth without my losing my nose. Part two was reconstruction. I was really scared before I went into the second surgery and I couldn't figure out why. It was quick reconstruction – an hour. But, during recovery, I felt myself slipping away to my right when all of a sudden I was shaking violently – inside. I struggled to come out of the anesthesia, and when I could finally talk, I asked the nurse what had happened and she said all went well, no problems. "I was shaking?" She said no. I was quiet as a mouse. I then asked the anesthesiologist and he said, no shaking – quiet as a mouse. Then, I remembered, there were several people at the end of my bed all dressed in white and a beautiful woman gently holding onto my legs. But – the recovery room staff were all dressed in blue. What happened? I was having my third near-death experience. Why?

It is now November 23, 2020, and I am finally getting some clarity on what I am supposed to do with these extraordinary connections. I am to share them with you. Heaven is REAL. Angels are REAL. They want you to know that they are here for you, every moment of every day. They want my experiences to help others see that there is another world outside of the massive changes that are taking place globally with Covid, race issues, Earth changes, and political and economic turmoil. They are asking me to share what I have learned over 40 years so that you can connect with the all-loving, all-supportive, non-physical realm of our world. So, just a glimpse into our world from the angelic perspective, here are some of the "Divine Dialogues" I have had over the years and now, every day:

- YOU ARE EXTRAORDINARY! Your soul chose to be here on earth, at this time, to help bring enormous change to our world.
- The catalyst for this change is – LOVE!
- All beings are sacred – animals, human beings, Mother Nature – even your plants and minerals. Love them all!
- Your life is a gift of TODAY, not regrets of yesterday or worries of tomorrow. Breathe life NOW, live life NOW, love life NOW!
- How important is your anger? If you could never hug or talk to that other person that you are angry with, would you still be angry at them? Once you have crossed to the other side, there is no going back. There are no hugs, no touching, no physical loving.
- Simplify, simplify. What are your true necessities in this world? How much "stuff" do you need? Maybe the less fortunate could use your "stuff" to stay warm or dressed. We are all energetically connected whether from Utah or Uganda.
- Be STILL sometime during your day for 10 minutes. Find gratitude in your heart for all in your life that gives you joy. Forget the challenges, they are learning cycles. Concentrate on the people, animals and events that give you joy. Hug a human, hug a horse!

These messages above are just a few of what I have received over the last 40 years and more importantly, in the last year. I have more angelic insights in my blogs on my website: www.SuePighini.com.

Why did I have three three near-death experiences? Because I volunteered to be a messenger of the heart. Welcoming change and inviting personal growth is my passion and purpose for being here. It is the human drive to find your deep desire for discovering your passion and purpose and to share it with others. Our passion connects us to our God.

I send each of you love and light during this extraordinary time of challenge and change. Namaste' – the divine in me sees the divine in you.

Sue Pighini Texas

Author of the Award-Winning Book 'EXPECT THE EXTRAORDINARY'

Motivational Speaker and Transformational Life Coach and Leadership Seminar Trainer

POOL OF PEACE

By Emilie Spear

May 4, 2012. The nurse added 1,270 mls to the white board by the door, almost tripling the amount of blood that had been lost. My dear husband's eyes shifted from being calm to outright fearful. I looked at the beeping machine and saw the blood pressure numbers falling and that my heart rate was extremely low. How could I still have any consciousness? I could see a group of doctors huddled together looking concerned and rather confused. The nurses scrambled to get yet another blood transfusion into my body, as they called for "Four more pints of blood – immediately!" Terci, the nurse who had helped deliver our twin girls, was sitting next to me touching my shoulder, reassuring me as she switched one machine on and pushed a button on another. I felt tired. Really, really tired.

As I looked up at the clock to see how much time had passed, the numbers began to fade and turn white. I looked at Terci with concern and said to her, "The numbers are turning white on the clock. Everything is turning into a beautiful, shining white light." Strangely, this light was comforting and inviting. My body became heavy and rather pain-free. I turned my head towards the doctors, nurses, and my husband and saw bright iridescent silver strings attached to each person's head, radiating upward, and thought, Hmm, I wonder where they go? They seemed to pulse, and some were shining stronger and more brightly than others.

As they all scrambled around the light became brighter, more encompassing, and I was feeling more and more... at Home. A sense of Peace was washing over me, although I could still see that everyone around me appeared frantic. Terci whispered to me in a firm manner, "You stay with me. Hear me? You stay with me. I am not going to leave you." I noticed her silver shining string shone the brightest, and then my eyes softly closed. The last thing I heard was, "Drop her head below the heart...."

No time. No day. Nothing. Darkness.

Then suddenly, as if in a lucid dream, I was watching my entire life unfold before me like a movie. I saw where my kind generous care for friends, family members and complete strangers from the past had turned their life direction to the better. I saw how my simple smile could change a moment in someone's life so deeply. I also saw myself in conversation with others and their inner silent reactions. In some moments, I was shown the depth of their inner pain and my unconscious ways of relating that I had not understood before.

Who would have known the great impacts we have on each other? This personalized movie was revealing the subconscious underlay of my entire life. The memories shown to me had a theme, as if there was a particular message I was intended to learn. Hmm, what was the larger message? These memories showed my gifts, my strengths, my successes; where I had made mistakes and grown, and aspects I had not yet fully understood while connecting with other sentient beings. Upon reflection, I was grateful for the life I had and yet also felt I could have done better! To have loved with greater awareness. To have had the capacity to understand the subconscious underlay which would allow me to understand other people even more, to be softer with my words and gentler with my actions... to Love in greater capacity!

The movie seemed to end, and I began floating upward and across toward a pool of golden soft light. I gently sat down upon the warm airy bank in a comfortable meditative posture. My lighted body felt very relaxed and rather spacious like a wispy cloud. The more relaxed I became, the more the golden light radiated warmly, and a calming, peaceful and soothing essence enveloped me. I could melt here forever. I was safe. I was Home. I was okay. Eternal Peace.

Then, out of the corner of my eye, a gentle, soft ripple appeared in this golden pool. With a smile, I curiously thought, Hello. The golden energy rose higher out of the pool and met my thought with an equal curiosity and kindness. Both of our energy-thoughts merged and eventually dissolved back into this Pool of Peace as One. Once the energy returned to the Pool of Peace, a sensation of delicious calming love, harmony, and wholeness washed over me.

In response, another thought arose from my mind to the light, You are so warming and caring. The golden light energy gently stirred and arose out of the pool to meet my thought with enormous warmth and care. Slowly, our energies merged and gently fell back into the Pool of Peace as One. Then, in a sensation of wholeness, ease and flow washed over me. What playful energy this is! With a childlike curiosity, I consciously chose a thought. Let's laugh and be boastful and play! This energy-thought jetted out from my light body with joyfulness towards the golden pool.

Quickly, a whirl of energy burst from the water, playfully tossing, and turning and meeting every aspect of my excited energy-thought, to once again unite each aspect and dissolve back into the Pool of Peace as One. Once settled, a great JOY vibrated throughout my entire lighted being. The sensation was beyond measure. I had never felt so complete and happy. This must be Heaven! If this is Heaven, could this be God? If so, I'd better be good and ONLY offer good thoughts.

Yet, I felt incredibly Safe and really couldn't do anything "wrong." With courageous curiosity, I thought maybe I could try something "not so good" but not "terribly bad" to see what happens? Anyway, who's deciding what's "good" or "bad?"

So, I mustered up some tears and memories of deep sadness rooted in shame, crawled shyly to the edge, and dropped it into the Pool of Peace. I slowly sat back with my head down and tears falling from my eyes. A gentle, warm breeze wisped through me as if to offer me a gentle hug of assurance. As I slowly opened my eyes, a swirling, misty, soft, golden light arose with tenderness and care, and delicately touched every little hidden facet, including the darkest aspect of shame—which was fully embraced by this golden light... merging together and simply disappearing back into the Pool of Peace as One. The Pool was Still.

In reflection, I felt a lifetime's burden lifted from my heart, and my airy being became even more weightless and lighter. The sensation of love grew more and more strongly in my heart and all around me. I had never felt this abundant, complete unconditional Love before. I was falling in-Love like never before. But wait! What? To my amazement, I could see that this Pool of Peace was falling in-Love with me, too! There was an Invitation, asking me to release more and more.

I was Safe. This unconditional Love was showing me there was no such thing as "good" or "bad." In fact, the more I offered, the more encompassing Love was being generated all around me. This Love was magnetically pulling me towards the Pool of Peace, to become One.

The Invitation was to free myself and surrender the burdens of sorrow and suffering. This Love was so rapturous, blissful, and completely consuming me. I was losing any sense of self-identity.

With great gratitude, I offered energy-thoughts and feelings of guilt, laughter, regret, happiness, confusion, firm beliefs, hopefulness, worthlessness, attachments, aversions... each time, being fully met, dissolving more and more, falling more and more in-Love as One. Each aspect of identity was being transmuted back into pure Divine Love. My lighted body was disappearing ever so gently and softly, merging more and more into the golden light. It seemed there wasn't anything this Pool of Peace would not fully meet with compassionate love to make whole. However, there was one more thing left......

Would it accept... the darkest of the darkest...? Could this love be THAT merciful, nonjudgmental, and gracious? Could it accept anger with all the jagged edges of resentment and hatred? Dare I?

As if aware of my thoughts, the Pool of Peace answered, "Yes." I slowly stood up and abruptly threw angry and bitter thoughts to the center of the pool, with absolute conviction. As I wanted to be free of suffering, I knew I had to Surrender everything! As I stood there, the golden light rose high and sharply into the air, shocking me with its serrated edges and fierce determination. I stepped backward with uncertainty, wondering how this would end.

Its spiky points quickly moved to soften and meet every one of the sharp angles, cracks, crevasses, and frightening fragments of this raging energy-thought. The golden light quickly and precisely met every aspect - nothing was untouched. The energies merged, made whole again, and then dissolved back into the Pool of Peace as One. Not a single ripple could be seen.

Done. It was over. "I" sat down. Humbled.

A wave of enormous Peace washed over everything. My lighted body was disappearing, evaporating into the golden light. There was no separation. The all-encompassing unconditional compassionate Divine Love was everywhere. "I" became no-thing, Yet, I AM everything.

The Pool of Peace has all of "me." And, all that is "me" is the Pool of Peace. Oneness.

Suddenly, a bold Voice proclaimed, "This is Divine Love." The vibration of this Voice penetrated the air, tincturing all of known existence with Wisdom of how Divine Love transmutes every aspect of separation and suffering, returning any aspect of self-identity into Oneness with Grace.

My lighted body re-appeared again. However, this time I was PINNED in a meditative posture. I COULD NOT MOVE. My back was in a straight line and my head perfectly balanced with a string of silver light holding me in perfect placement. No movement. Not even a thought. Stillness.

An extremely bright Light from above came down and touched through my forehead between my eyes at the ajna center. A pure white-lighted star awakened inside my forehead. It had always been there, Eternally, waiting to be lit. Like unwrapping a gift, a package of transmissions, lifetimes of teachings, full understandings of Divine Love manifestations awakened within me.

Wow, what just happened? Then, "I" began to merge back into the Pool of Peace, again. This time, falling deeper and deeper, faster and faster, in-Love. More and more golden Light penetrating through every aspect of my being, no more thoughts, no aspect of consciousness, everything dissolving into the great abyss of Divine Love. Disappearing... Becoming One.

"MOM. MOM!"

My eyes opened to the beautiful face of my newborn daughter, Cora, as I was blissfully disappearing into the Eternal Divine Love. "Remember, YOU are my MOM. You promised me, YOU would raise me." I could see deep into Cora's eyes and the depth of her request. Her twin sister, Sonja, was standing beside her with sad eyes. "Yes, I remember the promise and your life has just begun." Many pathways appeared, showing how my daughters would be raised, with or without me. I could not bear any pathway other than the one as their mother.

Suddenly, I was floating above my physical body in a hospital bed. I could see the threads of silver light on top of the heads of the doctors and nurses. They led to the Pool of Peace. Terci's head was shining brightly, just as before, as she was praying to Jesus. I saw Jesus touching her shoulder and he looked at me with the most Loving eyes, melting my heart as he emanated this Divine Love I had experienced. He asked if I wanted to go back to my body.

I nodded, yes. With a smile, I whispered to Jesus, "I'm going to need some help getting back into that body. It's very weak. Dr. Rose has a very bright light. Can we work through Terci and her?" Jesus replied, "Yes. Trust. Take what you have learned and bring that forth to ALL that you touch." "Yes, I Promise."

The Pool of Peace and the image of my lighted star-lit forehead flashed before me. My sacred Promise was to continue to unwrap this star-lit gift sealed inside of me and to BE a living, breathing human, expressing to my best capabilities these teachings of Divine Love. Then, the life-movie of my prior life memories appeared. In that quick moment, I proclaimed, "I'm doing this differently from now on!"

All sorts of karmic ties began to unwind between relationships. People and events appeared and disappeared, and automatic emotional reactions evaporated out of my physical body. New concepts of responding with compassion were filling this image of "me." Old "contracts" between relationships were no longer needed. Personal desires and ancient hurts were healed and brought back to wholeness.

Oh, I see how this works! This type of personal healing must be done in order to grow beyond personal desires and bring forth expressions of Divine Love for ALL beings. It's a perfect Design! Gathering these new insights, I remembered that the Pool of Peace had no other "agenda" than to wait for an arising, to clearly see its shape and energy, and to meet it fully and completely— to bring all back into wholeness and dissolve into the Pool of Peace as One.

I remembered, after each dissolving, I was blessed with increasing lighted Love, Grace, and Joy—which penetrated through everything. In Divine Union, the distinction between me and the Pool of Peace merged into One. I was shown, no matter what is manifested, it can be met with Divine Love.

As all is One. Jesus said, "Time is Now. Trust."

With my heart packed full of gems, and my forehead to light the way, I closed my eyes and Trusted like never before... falling, falling, falling into darkness.... Oh, I hear Terci's voice. Where is she? I moved closer and closer as her voice became louder and louder. "Emilie, I'm right here. Come back. I'm not leaving you! Come back."

My eyes opened to her loving eyes. She said, "Ah, there you are!" She was my tether to find my way back. Several angels attended with care around her, and Jesus stood behind them with a twinkle in his eyes. I knew I had made it. I thanked Jesus and the angels.

Smiling at Terci, I said, "You are my Earth Angel. Thank you for believing in me." And she smiled with a great sigh of relief. Moments later, Dr. Rose was able to determine the cause of my physical ailment post-childbirth, which required emergency surgery, immediately. The most experienced surgeon was starting his shift and the operating room suddenly had an opening. During this surgery, I continued to unwrap further teachings of Divine Love.

Integration of this experience has slowly merged with my physical form over time. During that period, at times, I wished I could have gone back to the Pool of Peace to experience such Oneness and Divine Love because there were moments where human life seemed riddled with fear and separation. There were moments of confusion. However, memories of the soft eyes of Jesus and my Soul Promise kept me inspired to figure out how to integrate even more and bring this Heavenly experience of Divine Love into my physical human daily life.

At the tender age of two, one of Cora's first sentences was "Mom, are you going to die again?" Her words stopped me so suddenly, as if she had known about this intimate inner experience since birth! This confirmed to me that she did call me back. That is, her Love for me and my Love for her pulled me back. I turned to her beautiful face with a gentle smile and looked deeply into her blue eyes and whispered, "No, honey, I am here to stay. I LOVE you."

Before my seventh year "new birthday," Jesus came into my meditations and supported further integrations. Since then, many blessings of the presence of other beautiful souls have entered my life to deepen further integration. The golden light from the Pool of Peace taught me what it means to truly and unconditionally Love with all-encompassing Compassion for all beings. The practice of observing my inner arisings as they appear, seeing them as movements of energy, meeting them fully without judgment and unconditional Love, and watching them dissolve into wholeness, has continued to heal more and more aspects of my human life. Furthermore, as I have learned to love myself this way, my capacity to unconditionally Love other people, animals, and any energy that arises has increased. As a result, more joy, peace, calm and harmony flows through me with such Grace. I am certainly living my life very differently now.

More "gems" of Divine Love have been slowly unfolding within my mind in the most gentle, kind, and graceful ways, with perfect timing—like a blooming Eternal Rose. I Trust so fully. ALL is unfolding perfectly!

Furthermore, fear has decreased significantly with whatever arises before me. I can see now it is simply energy made by the golden light of Divinity, offering an opportunity to practice meeting it with Divine Love. Because of this direct experience, I know that LOVE can meet any energy, and that it is LOVE that heals, transmutes and dissolves back into Oneness.

When whatever arises is seen, met and cared for, then it is made whole again. All eventually rests in the Pool of Peace as One. To give Love is to Bathe in-Love with all things around. And from this point of view, there is no separation between Heaven and Earth – as Heaven is here – right now – waiting to be remembered.

Every Life is precious – and to Love in each moment of Life is our Greatest Joy.

In 2021, my life continues to unfold in surprising and magical ways. I enjoy writing and sharing these gems of Divine Love that are available at any moment of our everyday lives.

And when there is a precious moment when someone transitions out of the physical body, I hope to bring some ease to let them know: There is nothing to fear.

Trust, as Jesus said. Trust. The Greatest Love is waiting for your remembrance.

Thank you for listening, and many Blessings to you and all beings. Peace to All.

Emilie Spear, Denver Colorado

THE DIVINE REMEMBRANCE

Information Is Not Describable (but I will try)

by Susan Redwine

During My Near-Death Experience My Energy "Split"
and went off to different "places".
"Part" of My Souls Essence and Energy went
to Visit the "River of Life"
Where EVERY Thing Was ALIVE,
Dancing & Vibrating in the Most Amazingly Brilliant Colors
That I Had Never Witnessed on Earth.
I Was AWE Struck at the Stunning Beauty.
There Truly are No Words to Describe the
Brilliance and JOY of What I Was Witnessing,
Experiencing and One With!!
Another "Part" of My Souls Essence and Energy went

to Visit the Angels,

Who Were Singing in

Unity, Unconditional LOVE Throughout

the Universes, Planets and Galaxies.

Reverberating Throughout My Soul and Spirit.

Beyond ANY Thing I have Ever Heard Before or Since.

I Saw that Unconditional Love Was What Everything IS

Made Of, All Beings, Souls,

IT is An Energy that We are Never Apart From.

We ARE Sacred Geometry IN Motion.

A Part of My Energy & Essence went to Visit

The "Music of the Spheres"

ALL of US Singing in Unity & Harmony

Each a Unique Tone and Color,

Vibrating in An Orchestra of STUNNING

Divine & Angelic Sounding Music,

That is Beyond My Ability to Describe in

ITS Radiance and Intensity!!

Bringing Unconditional Love, Peace, Amity,

Friendship, Fellowship,

Solidarity, Cooperation, Understanding, Unity, Goodwill,

Concert and Oneness Throughout the Times & Multiverses.

Part of My Energy & Essence went to Experience

a Life Review at the "Akashic Field"

what is also Known as The "Hall of Records",

Where Each Souls Holy Book of Records is "kept"

Where Each Souls Lives are Recorded

(moment by moment)

Throughout The Ages and Times.

That is Why I Always Say,

You are Writing Your Book of Life..EVERYDAY.

When they say that "Your Life Flashes Before Your Eyes"

This is How the Information Came to Me,

In A Flash, As there Was No Time.

I Saw the Me's Throughout All Times Eternal.

I Saw All of the Other People and Souls

that had Ever Interacted with Me,

Through the Eyes of Unconditional Love and Divinity.

There was NO Judgement!!

Of Myself or Any Other.

I was able to SEE Everyone's Reasons for Incarnating

and How We Were Helping Each Other,

Although It May Not "Appear" that way

While in a Human Body.

I Saw other Possible or Probable outcomes to all of my choices.

All the While this Was Happening,

My Soul Energies Essence was On a Table,

Being Revamped

ReEnergized,

ReInvigorated and Healed,

By My Soul Group, who Has Always Been with Me

Here/ There, Throughout Eternity,

For My Return Back to Earth and To My Human Body.

I was Everywhere at Once,

Doing many different "things".

I became One with Everything and Still remained Me.

I "Merged" With My "Higher Self"

I Reunited with the Whole and Holy Me..

However, Upon Returning to Earth,

Only a "Part or Fragment" of Me Came back.

This Human Body Could Not "Contain"

the "ALL" of Me, or It would Blow Up!

Many who have NDE's see other Souls in "Heaven"

who are actually alive on Earth, and are shocked.

When I came back,

I could not bring back the ALL of Me,

because other aspects of me are having

other Experiences & this Human form could not contain the Brilliance of Our Full Selves.

My Highest Self is always guiding Me from Home.

While a "fragment" of My Essence is here on Earth,

Sharing this Experience.

My Whole Experience was Overwhelmingly

Mind Blowing in All I Saw & Experienced.

The Ecstatic Joy, Unconditional Love,

The Divine Remembrance & Information is not Describable, Although I try.

I have come to the Understanding and Knowledge

that My Experience, although it was most Definitely

for Me, was a type of Map of Remembrance and

what would Be Happening to

Others, although Unique to them,

When Experiencing an Awakening.

That I Willingly Allowed Myself to Be "Used"

for the Highest Good of the ALL.

An Agreement, that I Fought many times..LOL.

Upon Returning to My Body,

I was Given Messages for Me to Remember,

And to Share with Others on My Journey..

Thank You for Coming to the Earth During

these Amazing Times!!

Thank You For Your Bravery and Your Courage.

You ARE Capable & Powerful Beings!!

REMEMBER Your Greatness at ALL Times.

LOVE IS the ANSWER,

ALL Ways & ALWAYS

Susan Redwine, Franklin, North Carolina is an Empath, Chef, Artist, Lover of Souls and a Freelance Writer who shares her Near-Death Experience with an intent to bring peace to those whose loved ones have passed and are experiencing grief about leaving the physical and transforming back into Spirit, as there is No Death, Only a Change of Worlds.

See Susan's full NDE story on television series LIFE TO AFTERLIFE #3 DEATH AND BACK available on Netflix and Hulu.

Palatable Lonesome

My journey may not be understood by those around me
this leap into the rabbit hole
holding an unquenchable thirst for more,
this drug of enlightenment, an addiction,
the relief shared to me piece by strategic piece
in nightly dreams and guided thought

Days are filled with a palatable 'lonesome' that spans the distance
between myself and others
feeling an awkward recipient of sensitivities,
and spiritual knowings,
a division
humanly real to the bone

But there is no un-knowing, nor the want of it,
there was only the moment of the choice to know,
and using free-will, the choice was mine to make

I do not walk alone
though in the depths of my humanness
and with exasperation
I will often look to the sky
for something that I do not yet see

Claudia Watts Edge

Chapter Two

OUR MILITARY BROTHERS AND SISTERS IN HEAVENS ARMS

This section is dedicated to our Brothers and Sisters serving in the Military.

Dying and coming back is enough cause for confusion, but dying in uniform and coming back leads a soldier to pause in what can be shared, and what should be held tightly within. An open exchange of the miraculous can be cause for dismissal, demotion, and dishonor and possibly the brig or padded walls. The phrase '*gap in care*' in many of the stories in this collection, is used in an effort to bring awareness to the needs of further education in the medical field in the arena of the Near-Death Experience.

MY MOMENT IN ETERNITY

By Tony Woody

One day when I was about nine years old I was playing near one of the ponds on our property in Elkhart, Texas. I was squatting next to the water's edge at the shallow end of the pond, antagonizing the tadpoles and crawdads, poking at them with a stick while they swam near the edge of the water.

Right behind me was a slight embankment covered in thick grass and weeds, and suddenly all the hairs on the back of my neck stood up and I instantly knew without a doubt that my life was in immediate danger.

I heard a loud but calming voice in my head that instructed me to, "Be calm, and move very slowly and you will not be harmed." At the same time that I heard the voice, I also had an absolutely clear vision of a large dark snake in my mind's eye sitting directly behind me all coiled up and ready to strike. I followed the instructions and did not panic.

I slowly leaned forward while placing most of my weight on my left hand in the mud at the water's edge. I slowly turned my head around to look back over my right shoulder. Those few extra inches of space I created by leaning to my left away from the snake saved my life, because as I looked over my right shoulder there sat a big fat and very poisonous water moccasin staring right at me with those evil dead looking snake eyes. I froze with fear for an instant knowing full well he was about to strike.

When I saw the mouth on the snake beginning to open slightly, I heard a clear command to "Run!" and I bolted out into the water away from the snake as fast as I could. I did not look where I was going, instead, I kept my eyes laser focused on the snake as it began its attack. I saw his mouth flying wide open as he launched his strike at me. When I bolted to my left to get away from it, time suddenly slowed way down. I could see everything happening in a surreal kind of slow-motion scenario. My awareness level and attention to detail was incredible.

I could see the snake's head with its cotton white mouth wide open sporting two awfully long hypodermic needle like fangs hurtling straight at me. I was staring eye to eye with the snake right before it launched its strike, and again I heard a powerful Command in my head that did not come from me, and it said one word. "RUN!" I wasted no time reacting to that Command. I bolted away as fast as I could while my eyes were laser-locked on the snake that was coming straight at me.

The strangeness of the clarity of that moment has never left me and just when I thought I would feel the fangs sink into my face, I saw the snake's head snap to a halt as his body became fully extended. He had reached the maximum range of his strike ability and had barely missed me. I had the strange sense that I was being watched over and protected. There was the feeling of a Presence that I cannot explain in mere words, but I knew it was there, this Magic Presence felt remarkably familiar to me, and I have never forgotten that feeling of protection. At the time I didn't understand what that was, but today I know beyond any doubt whatsoever, that was God watching over me.

After I felt part of the snake's jaw brush my right shoulder area as his body recoiled from the force of the strike. He had barely missed hitting me in my face, and I swear I don't think Christ had anything on me when it came to walking on water because I shot across the thirty-foot pond so fast I don't think my feet ever got a single drop of water on them.

Due to adrenalin and fear I was unsure if I had been bitten at all, and I needed to know for sure. I ran to the house and straight to the bathroom mirror to see if I had bite marks anywhere. Once I realized I was okay I did what most kids would do. I shrugged it off and went outside to play again. Just not down by the water this time.

As a kid I didn't stop to think about the depth of the potential ramifications of a life-threatening moment like that, so I never had any bad dreams about it afterwards that I can remember. But at the same time, I never forgot the strangeness of the event. For years I wondered "how in the world could I have known that snake was sitting behind me like that and was about to strike?" I was filled with questions of how could I have "seen" that snake in the grass when I wasn't even looking at it? Or, How could time slow down like that? Where did that calming but commanding Voice in my head that told me not to make any sudden moves come from? It had told me to run at exactly the right moment. Who was the Voice? And finally, what exactly happened to me that day?

It would take more than three decades to get my answers.

My name is Tony Woody and I'm a retired US Navy Chief Petty Officer with 22 years of honorable military service. I was an Instructor Flight Engineer on the P3 Orion and EP3 Orion aircraft for twenty years logging over ten thousand flight hours. I also held a top secret security clearance while flying sensitive missions in the EP3 aircraft.

The P3 Orion is a 71-ton, four-engine heavyweight turbo-prop aircraft designed for long range maritime patrol missions.

One does not have to physically die to have a Near-Death Experience (NDE) or to have a Near-Death Like Experience (NDLE). The psychological and emotional after-effects caused by an NDLE are identical to those experienced by someone declared clinically dead whether the body physically dies or not.

People who have crossed the veil and returned are called "Experiencers." As an Experiencer, I lived in spiritual crisis with a moral injury for decades. I needed help but never got any because I wasn't believed by anyone I tried to talk with about what happened to me. These "Experiences" are happening to soldiers around the world while in combat or during some other non-combat, traumatic event like what happened to me during an emergency engine-out landing that didn't go well causing our plane to depart the runway and somehow triggering an Out of Body Experience. That means the number of people being clinically affected after an NDE or NDLE type event is far higher than currently understood or believed. That alone makes this an enormous military readiness concern, not to mention a huge concern for front line providers and clergy as well.

After I had my "Experience" in the Light, I urgently needed help understanding what exactly happened to me but got no answers, subsequently causing a moral injury causing me to live in spiritual crisis mode for over two decades without any real professional help. That is the essence of the "Gap in Care" problem that's unknowingly creating moral injuries. Something must be done to bring more awareness to this problem, ergo my primary reason for sharing my story.

Unbeknownst to me for many years, my "Gap in Care" moral injury and subsequent NDE aftereffects affected my ability to maintain proper military readiness, even though I hid it well from everyone, including myself, until I couldn't. I didn't even know I was struggling with NDE aftereffects for years. All I knew was I desperately needed help finding answers of what exactly happened to me that day, but instead, due to this "Gap in Care" culture, I got no help at all. I can assure you there are many more people out there suffering emotionally with profound psychological NDE aftereffects than just people who physically died in a medical emergency and were resuscitated. For that very reason I made a video at the following link discussing the psychological impact of NDE Aftereffects.

https://www.youtube.com/watch?v=p3aAk8AKRQg.

Here's what happened. In 1982 during an emergency engine-out landing at Naval Air Station Barbers Point in Hawaii, the aircraft suddenly departed the runway at 135 knots (just over 155MPH) due to pilot error almost immediately after the pilot initiated reverse thrust after landing the plane. We narrowly missed slamming into a firetruck that was prepositioned a mere 100 feet away off the right-hand side of the runway. The moment I realized my death was just seconds away was the most helpless, hopeless, and terrifying moment I have ever known, and it caused a raw, visceral terror within me that somehow triggered a spontaneous Out of Body Experience (OBE). I wasn't dead, I wasn't injured or unconscious, I wasn't on drugs, I wasn't low on oxygen, I wasn't anything like that. I was wide awake doing my job when it happened to me, making it absolutely impossible for me to assume it was caused by an injury or any other reason that made sense to me.

Right before the OBE started my perception of reality suddenly changed. Time slowed way down, and I began experiencing this distinct and clear sense of my consciousness being located in two different places inside and outside the airplane at the same time. I was totally confused and desperately trying to understand what was happening to me. I was stunned at how much went through my mind when I knew I only had a few precious seconds left to live. Nothing in my twenty-two years of military training ever prepared me for anything like that. It absolutely rocked my world and changed my life forever.

My OBE in the plane was followed by a full-blown Spiritually Transformative Experience (STE) just two days later in my bedroom. When that happened, I instantly understood I was in the presence of my Creator. I saw and felt God eternally and infinitely expressing divine Light, Purity, Power, Perfection, Knowledge, Wisdom and Unconditional Love on a cosmic scale. It poured out everywhere, in all directions, and I was One with all of it. I am blessed to have personally witnessed the genesis of "all of creation and all that exists" (I don't know how else to say it), coming straight from the eternal Unfed Heart Flame of my Mighty "I AM" Presence. Apparently, I caused that to happen myself after saying a simple little silent prayer in my head two days after the aircraft incident. I still don't understand how, but my Out of Body Experience during the aircraft incident opened some kind of a "spiritual doorway" in my bedroom while I was sleeping.

Two days after the aircraft incident I was at home relaxing with my wife and son, watching a TV show called "That's Incredible." This particular episode was about a man named Leslie Lemke who was totally blind and severely mentally disabled. Leslie spontaneously and miraculously became a singing savant pianist though he never had any singing or piano lessons. While watching the show I knew in my heart I was seeing a miracle. That night I said a silent prayer before falling asleep. That little prayer profoundly changed my life forever and went like this. "Dear Lord, thank you for letting me see my first miracle on the TV tonight. It would be nice if you could do something like that for me someday."

I will never underestimate the power of prayer again because that prayer set my life on a path I never saw coming. While I was sleeping all of a sudden with no warning whatsoever, BOOM, I had an instantaneous shift in the location of my consciousness. I was experiencing the essence of the Being I know to be God and I was dumbfounded by how insanely in Love with me God is. I had no idea Love could be like that, no idea at all. I was instantly overwhelmed and stunned beyond cognitive ability with God's Love. It felt like I was God's most important concern in the entire Universe at that moment while being enfolded in God's divine Love and Peace in the void, the "Great Silent Chamber," where I was somehow allowed to be "One" with God and all of Creation.

God's personal feelings were powerfully and harmoniously flowing through the very essence of my being. I knew God, and God knew me, and there's no such thing as separation while in the Presence of God.

The astonishing glorious beauty of God's Light and depth of emotions within the void, which was fully enfolding and enveloping my own emotions, is forever seared into my consciousness. I no longer fear death because of my Experience. I'm not saying I'm looking forward to the process of dying, but I'm not afraid of what comes after death. That's because I know God's divine Light, Love, Purity, Perfection, and Beauty that I witnessed pouring out in all directions, filling and enfolding the very essence of my soul with living Light and Love, will be waiting for me when I die. I've witnessed the Unfed Flame of living liquid molten golden-white Light coming straight from God's own Heart creating, expanding, and infinitely expressing divine Love to all of God's children and Creation forever.

Clearly that Experience rocked my world. I desperately needed help afterward because of something called "NDE aftereffects" that get exacerbated when a "Gap in Care" event occurs, usually due to untrained first responders, clinical providers, or clergy personnel who don't even know what an NDE or NDLE is; ergo their collective ignorance regarding NDE aftereffects institutionally speaking. Many first providers are unwittingly and unintentionally inflicting moral injuries due simply to their ignorance of the NDE phenomena and its aftereffects. The need for a standardized training program regarding NDE or NDLE types of experiences is immense.

Hopefully my testimony will lead to a better protocol designed specifically to help front line providers clinically identify and recognize NDE and NDLE symptoms and aftereffects without judging, stigmatizing, or assuming mental illness or some other potentially errant diagnosis first. A front line provider's reaction to what a patient is saying about their hyper-fresh NDE will have a lifelong psychological impact one way or the other.

The quickest way to lose your security clearance, job, and military career is to tell someone with authority over your career you personally met God. I learned that early on after being warned by a Navy Lieutenant Commander, my pastor, and essentially my wife as well, when all of them made it clear in their own individual ways that I had better stop talking about it. So I did for over 20 years, and as I've said many times since, that was a big mistake. In that window of time I struggled with alcohol, divorced my wife, lost my family, and basically had a really hard time. I became angry but did not understand the source of my anger for decades. Feeling betrayed by everybody, I quickly learned not to talk about my experience in order to avoid the stigma of mental illness and protect my military security clearance so I wouldn't lose my flight engineer job and Navy career I loved so much. Over time I realized I was going to have to figure out what really happened to me on my own. I felt all alone for a very long time, all the while wondering if I was the only one who knew God is real. Unwittingly I made my moral and psychological injuries worse when I resolved not to talk about it ever again.

I describe my experience with God in this 23 minute long video showing the power and depth of the emotional impact it still has on me decades later whenever I tell my story.

https://www.youtube.com/watch?v=vijNhS1DuSU&t.

My suffering was completely unnecessary due to the culture that still exists today in clinical, clergy, and first responder settings. This "Gap in Care" problem is unwittingly inflicting both moral and psychological injuries that are scarring people for life every day. I know that's true because I lived it. Initially all I really needed was validation.

After decades of seeking spiritual validation, my moral injury was healed using the Saint Germain Series "I AM" Instruction which contain the Original Instruction from the Ascended Masters on the Eternal Laws of Life. Each Book and Discourse carries the definite Radiation and Consciousness of the Ascended Masters and points the Student to the attainment of the Ascension through their use of the Sacred Fire. This Mighty "I AM" Instruction is the True Education of Life. It is the Law of Life and the Gift of Love!

The answers I had been looking for actually found me when a lovely lady named Lilia contacted me and told me about the Saint Germain Foundation, or else I would still be looking for my answers to this day. Lilia introduced me to the Saint Germain Series "I AM" Instruction books that contain the Original Instruction from the Ascended Masters regarding the Eternal Laws of Life, and point the Student to the attainment of their own Ascension through their constructive use of that Sacred Fire that I personally experienced and witnessed in the void of the Great Silent Chamber where I was allowed to kneel at the Alter of the Sacred Fire of Eternal Love in the Throne Room of Creation where I experienced Oneness with all the Is.

Before I started studying these books I had relentlessly researched dozens of religions and read thousands of books on spirituality trying to learn who and what I truly am. After over thirty fruitless years seeking my answers I finally found them in the Saint Germain Series "I AM" Instruction books. They're the only books I ever found calling the Light the "Great Central Sun" while describing the Love, Light, and everything I saw and felt exactly like I personally experienced in the Throne Room of Creation where I saw and felt the divine Love pouring out in all directions from the Heart of the "Love Star" firsthand. After that Experience I knew the spiritual standard and Truth that I was looking for all those years and I was not willing to accept anything that didn't meet those standards even if it meant seeking fruitlessly for the rest of my life. No other books I read ever called what I saw by that name, but that's exactly what it is. The "Love Star" is God's Heart eternally creating and expanding Love throughout the Universe, forever. Everything in the Universe, including all Life, is made with divine Love and Light. It can be no other way. Now, all we have to do is go be Love, forever.

I found all of my answers at the Saint Germain Foundation https://www.saintgermainfoundation.org/ and the "I AM" Instructions books can be found at https://www.saintgermainpress.com/books /saint-germain-series/ .

The Saint Germain Foundation and the "I AM" Instructions are not a religion, even though many might think they are. These books are actually instructions on how to achieve our own Ascension. I have practiced these principles for many years now I've had and am still having powerful Spiritual Experiences along with others around me who have co-experienced some of these experiences right along with me at the same moment in time. Because of these books and the results I have been having that are undeniably God overtly acting in my life, I have stopped "seeking" answers anymore. Now I solely study and practice the "I AM" Instructions from the Saint Germain Foundation. I highly recommend and believe all of mankind must do the same at some point. God bless America.

Tony Woody, Exeter NH

US Navy Chief Petty Officer, retired, with 22 years of honorable military service. I was an Instructor Flight Engineer on the P3 Orion and EP3 Orion aircraft for twenty years logging over ten thousand flight hours.

See more of Tony's story on the series LIFE TO AFTERLIFE #3 DEATH AND BACK available on Hulu and Netflix.

MUTINY: LISTENING TO MY INTUITION

by Reverend Bill McDonald Jr.

In 1967, about 35 miles northwest of Saigon, I had to make one of the biggest decisions of my life. We had been flying solo missions, mostly supply runs to small encampments of the 1st Infantry Division. The troops were there to slow down the movement of supplies that were coming directly from North Vietnam off the Ho Chi Minh Trail. Our intelligence reports indicated that we should be on the lookout for large movements of both supplies and troops coming into this sector.

My helicopter commander was a brand-new major who had just arrived in Vietnam from several years in Germany. He was a West Point graduate. When he gave an order, he expected a full 100 percent obedience by those he commanded. We knew he wouldn't be open to any questions or suggestions.

On this particular morning, we were flying higher in the sky (over 800 feet) than felt comfortable to me. We were not at our normal treetop-level altitude. The major had an aversion to flying too close to the ground. He did not yet realize the risks that flying at higher altitudes presented. Eventually, he would learn—like all new pilots did—that flying at treetop level was actually much safer. We could sneak up on enemy troops well before they could see or hear us coming; this was the common procedure in Nam—fly low and fast.

From our loftier position in the sky, we could see much farther around the countryside. I think it may have been helpful for him in spotting landmarks for his navigation. We did have a greater view of all that was down below, but it also made us an easier target. We were not high enough to avoid small arms fire and not low enough to sneak up on anyone. We just kind of hung in the sky like a big fat, slow moving target.

We were flying just a kilometer outside of a small hamlet, when I spotted a group of about 30 people below us who appeared to be moving down the road in a military formation. They were all carrying what looked like some kind of weapon on their shoulders. There also was a man in the front who seemed to be acting as a leader for the group. They were all dressed in the typical black pajamas that the VC wore. Since this was so close to the Ho Chi Minh Trail, it certainly appeared that it could be a good-sized squad of VC (Viet Cong).

The major immediately determined that they were VC troops— he had no doubts. He ordered me to fire my M-60 machine gun on the formation below. Now, my M-60 could fire 750 rounds of 7.62 mm of ammo a minute—it would have shredded that group of people in just a matter of a few seconds. I looked down at the formation and thought what he saw was correct, but then I froze. I couldn't pull the trigger on the machine gun. I could not get myself to squeeze off a single round. I was overcome with great apprehension and a feeling that something was not right. My intuition said STOP – something is NOT right!

I sat behind my M-60 doing nothing. The major was going crazy and yelling orders at me. He let me know that he had given me a direct order to fire. It was not optional. But I just sat there, knowing that something was not right with this picture. I told the major I was not going to fire. I had some heavy doubts about what we were seeing down on the road.

The major could not believe that I had actually questioned his orders. He was mad as hell. He told me that I had disobeyed a direct order in combat. That was a punishable offense. He let me know, in no uncertain terms, that he was going to bring me up on charges. Those charges could mean 20 years or more in a military prison at Leavenworth.

I told him that we needed to fly lower. I wanted him to make a pass over the group's formation so we could get a better identification. In the meantime, he had circled the aircraft so that the left door gunner was directly in line to fire his weapon on those on the ground. To my surprise, the door gunner also refused the order to shoot. He showed some exceptional courage by supporting my position. He fully understood what he had just done, and that took my breath away. He was certainly not looking for any trouble from the major, but there he was making a stand with me on this issue. It would have been viewed as a mutiny by the military court system. This was a serious breach of military law, and we each could have been facing life sentences. I was in awe that he had such courage and conviction, and he was basing it on his belief in my feelings. I hoped to God that I was right, for both of our futures. That was a lot of weight on my shoulders.

The major was debating with the copilot, a young warrant officer from Texas, about calling in an air strike or at least some artillery. The young pilot, who had flown with us many times before, suggested that we take the aircraft down for a closer look. Finally, we dropped down from our higher altitude and made a descent toward the group of people on the ground. We had our M-60 machine guns at the ready position, aiming right at the heart of the group.

We came down to about 100 feet. We were unsure of what to expect and were ready for all hell to break loose as we passed off to the right side of them. The first clue we had that they might not be the enemy was the fact that they stayed on the road the whole time we were above them. They had not run into the cover of the surrounding jungle. The second clue was that no one was firing at us as we passed by them at only 100 feet in the air.

As we flew across the road, it became painfully obvious to all of us who they were; this was just a group of school age children with their garden tools, marching in a formation to the community garden. The leader was a priest dressed all in black. My heart raced; I got all emotional and actually felt tears rolling down my face. I realized just how close we had come to killing all these young children.

I couldn't see the major's face, but I imagined that it turned pale. All of us onboard were visibly shaken by this event. The major had given direct orders to both his gunners to kill them all. He even wanted to order an air strike on this group of 30 children. Now, he said very little. I had chills running down my spine and noticed that my hands were shaking.

Why had I and my trusting door gunner both refused to fire? I have no answers. I went with my feelings, which at the time were so very clear and strong that I should not pull the trigger. I risked going to jail because I followed my feelings and not my orders. What if I had been wrong and they were really VC? I had risked the helicopter getting shot down and the life of every crew member—based only on my feelings. I quickly learned in Nam to never question my intuitive feelings. It seemed that those feelings were greatly heightened in combat and dangerous situations. In this case, it saved 30 young children and a priest from being killed. That would have been a major tragedy that I could never have lived with because it would have haunted me for the rest of my life. I learned that day to always listen and trust my inner voice.

Rev. Bill McDonald is Keynote Speaker & Workshop Facilitator for The IANDS 2019 Conference. He is an author, award winning poet, minister, national veteran advocate, film advisor, artist, motivational speaker, and leader and founder of Spiritual Warrior Ministries

CHASING THE LIGHT

By Chase Skylar DeMayo

I died while serving in the United States Air Force, April 1, 2008. I remember waking up that morning—well after I had hit the snooze button a few times. I had been late to work several times recently. Our Public Affairs Office had merged with another unit on Langley Air Force Base, and my new supervisor and I did not mesh well at all. I knew my time in the Air Force was ending soon due to the unsuccessful knee surgery I had undergone the year prior. I was 21 years old, with a huge chip on my shoulder.

From seventh grade on, I was determined to be one of America's elite fighting machines. A hero. An Airman. After suffering a knee injury, retraining to be a journalist, being stuck in an office, forced to use a cane and crutches, and then being told the knee surgery was not a success... I was bitter. I was angry. I had stayed away from drugs, stayed out of trouble in school, graduated, got myself in incredible shape, sold my car, and lost touch with friends from home in order to dedicate myself to the military for life. At 21 and away from home, no one was there to set me straight.

By April 2008, the door was closing on my lifelong Air Force dreams. But I had no clue what I was going to do when that time came. I looked at the alarm clock that Tuesday morning and decided it was time to get my uniform on and head to the office to face my supervisor, who I knew was waiting to reprimand me, but as I got up, my mind went blank.

My next memory was being at the Langley Air Force Base Emergency Center, lying flat on my back, with a nurse going through her routines. The doctor came to visit me in the last bed on the hall, a small room with a wall to my right and a curtain to my left, where the machines beeped continually.

The doctor let me know they didn't know why I was unconscious on the floor of my dorm, so they wanted to run some tests. All of my vitals were good, so they would check my head for any damage from the fall and would perform a spinal tap to see if blood entered my spine, as well as a routine chest X-ray.

The nurse checked-in periodically to let me know they hadn't forgotten about me. She said they would discharge me soon, because, so far, there was nothing wrong with the test results coming back. When the doctor returned to my bed, he said it made no sense why a perfectly healthy 21-year-old was found lying unconscious on the floor. With no history of drug use, drinking, or smoking, and a commitment to a healthy diet, he said the best bet was to send me home and call what had happened a "fainting spell."

My health at the time was at its peak. I frequented the gym regularly—sometimes twice a day. I logged my foods. I was the healthiest I had ever been. It was more for vanity at the time, but, nonetheless, they couldn't blame those things. They were going to update my IV and bring over a mobile chest X-ray machine, which was the final test before sending me on my way. After adjusting my IV, the nurse left my room.

Suddenly, things started to slow down. I started to feel dizzy. It wasn't a regular dizziness — it was a type of dizziness that felt like I was shedding gravity. While lying flat on the bed, I felt like the room had slowly started to distort, get foggy, and brighten. An alarm started, sounding from what I assumed was my room. At this point, my hearing and vision started to pulse in and out like waves in an ocean.

I vividly remember the look of the female nurse when she came running back into my room. A look of terror, concern and confusion filled her eyes. She looked at my face, then studied the vitals monitor to my left side. Within seconds, another nurse sprinted into my room. Another nurse came barreling in after him. They were followed by a doctor, who I remember almost running into the wall past my room, as if his brakes didn't work, like a Looney Tunes cartoon character.

Everything was in slow motion, but was also moving so fast at the same time. Everything was so loud, but also so quiet. My vision seemed to double, but I had never seen so clearly. It seemed in those moments that I could experience the nurses and doctors' feelings of fear and confusion. I could feel their hearts pounding, while mine seemed to be nonexistent. I laid silently in the bed, witnessing the doctors and nurses shouting to each other, taking turns staring me directly in the eyes, then staring at the monitor. I was watching them watch me die.

In all of the chaos, a man appeared, sat to my left, and began to hold my hand. He started to stroke my arm with his other hand, which sent a sensation of calm through my entire body. The sensation of calm was combined with goosebumps. Who was this man? I tried to look over at him, but he gently stopped my chin from turning. He said as clear as a needle dropping in absolute silence, "Everything is okay. Be calm."

I thought, how can I hear him so clearly while I also hear the terror of the medical staff surrounding me? I tried to look at him again while he held and stroked my hand. Don't look this way right now," he said, "There is air traveling up your arm right now, and it's going to hurt a little. They are trying to save you."

Before I could comprehend what he meant, I felt extreme pain. I can still feel this pain today when I think of my experience, and I can only describe it as the most excruciating pain I have ever felt. It felt like a cold silver bullet traveling a direct path from my left wrist up my arm to my heart. I looked again at the scared eyes of the nurses and doctors above me and then tried to turn again to the left to see the man who had brought me calm and peace while I felt this pain. He tried again to gently stop my chin from looking all the way over, but this time, I persisted.

I turned my head all the way to my left. Then I saw it. At that moment, I watched my heart monitor line beep and fall completely flat. The sign of a dead heart.

Except I did not die. I was born.

As soon as I saw the monitor, I knew what it meant. I could feel everything besides pain or fear. Instead of closing your eyes and seeing darkness, I saw light, and my chest felt like it was being pulled by the brightest light you could ever imagine. It was brighter than white. It's not fair to give it a color, because it was a feeling.

The light came through my body and pulled me so quickly and beautifully that I can only describe it as pure bliss. My entire heart felt like it was filled with the coldest ice you can imagine, and my body felt no gravity, no pain, no confusion, no sadness. Everything in that moment made sense to me. There was no fear. It felt like I was remembering that this had been the plan all along.

As I was pulled through this light, I was surrounded by a circling tunnel. The tunnel didn't have walls or a boundary. The tunnel seemed to be formed by swirling wings of energy flying around me, creating this cold, windy sensation that made me feel like the wings were carrying me upwards. I felt amazement and almost laughed while watching what looked like shooting stars darting past me and around me, circling me.

There was a sound of melodic bells and twinkles, while my body was completely forfeited to this light that was a vehicle to wherever I was going. The music sounded like angels and fairies hitting small bells or wind chimes ringing from the wind of angels' wings. If smiling could be a musical instrument, that's what this music sounded like. There's nothing on Earth to compare it to.

At some point, while taking in all this beauty, I realized I was standing in what felt like a garden. But calling it a garden is unfair. This was the most beautiful picture, which could never be painted, even with colors that don't exist. But this was indeed a garden with dirt, grass, trees, flowers, and a perfect blue sky. The flowers looked like flowers, but they were not of this world. The dirt below me was dirt indeed, but wiggling your toes in this dirt felt like therapy.

While enjoying the magnificence of this garden, I saw a man and a child walking in the distance ahead of me. Just focusing on them seemed to bring me closer to them without needing to walk or travel their direction. The man was dressed in a perfectly clean white robe. His hands were tucked behind his back while he casually strolled with this little boy. The little boy looked to be about four years old and had golden curls past his ears, chubby cheeks, and a smile that gave the impression he was a bit mischievous. The man in the robe had short, dark brown hair in tight curls, piercing green eyes, and a thin nose.

The man in the robe leaned over to the little boy and gave him a pat on his shoulder. The little boy started to run ahead, laughing and looking back, exactly like a cheeky kid would do at a park or playground. I felt a sense of love and pride as the man laughed back at the little boy.

When the man in the robe turned to me, it hit me. I realized instantly that the man in the robe was the man who was holding my hand at the hospital. It was at that moment that I knew with 100 percent certainty that I was standing with Jesus in that garden. There was no guessing, no assuming. If you look today in the mirror and recognize yourself, that's the feeling of recognizing Jesus. He looked nothing like what I had grown up seeing him as. Nothing like what I saw in Catholic school. Nothing like any statue or symbol or poster I had seen. But I knew without a doubt that it was Jesus standing with me in that very moment, just as if I had been standing with someone I had seen a thousand times before.

He could clearly see the gears turning in my head, and he let out a chuckle. Grinning, he knew that I was starting to realize what was happening and where I was. I start to connect the dots of him being next to me in the hospital, me watching myself die, and me watching him play with this boy in the garden.

We both looked back at the little boy who had run ahead, and I immediately felt a wave like cold ice hit me again. I recognized that little boy: It was me. I never think of myself with gold hair. When I think back to myself as a little boy, I picture myself with dark brown hair, slicked back, because my grandma said that was what the guys did in soap operas. Until I was five, however, I had bright golden curly hair that my grandparents had made sure I had grown out into a trendy 90's mullet. The little boy was me. I was watching myself play in a garden with Jesus.

In that moment, it was all real. It was all very real. Not only was it real, but it also made sense. I can best describe what I felt was similar to Charles Dickens' "A Christmas Carol." I was standing with Jesus watching the happiest form of myself. A kid who had maybe four teeth in total, but also the biggest grin and a belly full of laughter.

I took it in and realized I was in Heaven, watching what happiness was. We didn't exchange spoken words back and forth like a traditional conversation. The joy itself seemed to be the conversation; the light and the love that was flowing through me was filled with information and memories.

Jesus turned to me and said with another smile on his face, "You have to go back now." I took another look around. I remember feeling content with his guidance—as if this was all part of the plan. "I need you to go back and remember to share laughter, joy, love, and light," he said. When he said those words, it was if they were being tattooed into me, or digested into my heart. Those words hit me like a truck.

Before I could respond, he started to grin again. It was the type of grin you have right before a laugh starts to come out. There was such a sense of fun and humor during my time spent in the garden. To me, it felt like the relationship you have with a best friend or sibling or spouse, where even the slightest notion could send you into peals of laughter. His grin was my last memory before gravity set in and the weight of the world started to set into my human body again. It was obvious I was no longer in Heaven, where everything was so free and weightless.

The hospital room I was in was much larger and much nicer, and no one was there when I opened my eyes. I closed my eyes again, hoping that I was dreaming and could just shut my eyes and go back. That didn't work. I kept trying to close my eyes again and again, until someone finally came into this new hospital room. We were not on the Air Force base anymore. I had been transported at some point during my journey off-base to a civilian hospital in another city in Virginia.

Other than feeling tired, I felt completely normal. I felt at ease. I felt like nothing was wrong with me. The civilian doctor came to visit and said they would discharge me. The Air Force was coming back to get me and return me to their hospital. However, I had other plans. I called friends in the area and jokingly told them that I had just died but I felt completely fine and had a craving for Chick-fil-A. I told them about my left arm and the air traveling up my vein. I made everything a joke, because I didn't have the time to process what had happened to me.

I went on Facebook that night and posted about how I had flat-lined in the hospital. Except I didn't realize it was April 2. An entire day had passed, and I had no clue. For the following two weeks after April 2, the Air Force conducted every heart diagnostic they could try on me... and found nothing. They sent me an email eventually and told me I had a healthy heart and that I should move on. It caused so much confusion for me at the time. How could I die, but no one know why or how?

What does a 21-year-old do after such a clear, defined, and transformative experience while in the Air Force? Nothing. I told no one about my experience. I joked about dying with friends, but I knew if I told anyone about my experiences in Heaven that they would think I was either crazy, lying, or both. I couldn't tell people I had met Jesus. Who was I to share that? A church might look at me and say, "He hasn't earned his right to enjoy such an experience." My friends and family might think it was all for attention. So, for 12 years, it stayed a secret from almost everyone but my close friends and family. Until now.

I can confidentially say that at 21 years old, if you had asked me what Heaven was like or who I'd meet—I would probably have said Elvis and that it would be filled with peanut butter and jelly sandwiches and milk.

Neither Jesus nor Heaven were a priority in my life at that time. I had never fantasized about dying and what that might be like. I didn't know about the term "Near-Death Experience" or that there was a world of similar survivors—until I was working aboard a Carnival Cruise ship, and a passenger approached me on the deck while the ship was docked in Jamaica. He gave me a nod and a smile and handed me a book called In Life, in Death, He Leads by Bruce Blair. Without saying a word, the man disappeared.

This book sits next to me every single day in my office, and I have purposely not read it. It has been more than six years since I was given the book, but I have only read the synopsis, which is based on this man's journey with surviving death and his experience with God. Why haven't I read it you may ask? I have wanted my Near-Death Experience (NDE) to be written from my heart and not be persuaded or guided by any other experiencer's journey. I have avoided reading more about NDEs and others' books for this reason. It is important for my story to be untainted or uninspired by anyone else but myself and my time spent with Jesus in the garden.

Through this journey, I have found just one painting of Jesus that truly depicts what he looked like when I died and what he looks like when I have the opportunity to see him periodically. Painter Akiane Kramarik painted The Prince of Peace at the age of eight. It is an exact, almost photographic, image of the man who reminded me to spread laughter and love.

For 12 years, I have silently felt others' joy and pain. For 12 years, I have been suppressing the strong intuition that was gifted to me. For 12 years, I have felt the presence of loved ones no longer in human form around strangers and have wanted so badly to give them encouragement in their journey. I am ready to share the gifts I was born with and the gifts that continue to strengthen since my Near-Death Experience on April 1, 2008. While I have spent the last 12 years spreading laughter and smiles with others, there are so many out in the world, like me, who have been terrified to share their own experiences. Now, I get to help others Chase the Light.

*After several requests for my records, the military is only missing two days of records out of my entire military service: April 1 and April 2, 2008. The records are gone, however, there are clear references still on my military records that document the event happening, including the terrible bruising up my left arm, being found on the floor, being transported to another hospital, and being discharged. Thankfully, there is proof of my death, but most of it has been deleted, for reasons unknown.

Chase Skylar DeMayo Orlando FL United States Air Force

Chase is a US Air Force Veteran who Died April 1st, 2008 and sent back to spread laughter, light, love, and joy with the world. Injured early in Survival Training in the Air Force, Chase became a Public Affairs Journalist where he had the opportunity to share his stories with active duty military and supporters. After a Near-Death Experience through cardiac arrest in 2008 while stationed at Langley Air Force Base, Chase kept his Near-Death Experience private in fear of judgement and retribution for twelve years until now. Since being medically retired from the Air Force in 2008, Chase has worked in television, radio, sports entertainment, comedy writing and also performing at theme parks and national events. In October 2020, Chase attended a Veteran's Mental Health Retreat which reopened his Near-Death Experiences and created a newfound passion to helping fellow veteran's and their supporters.

A LIFE WORTH LIVING

A Civil War Medic finds Healing in this Lifetime

By Gregg Untenberger

"**O**h God. Oh, dear God, no!" he said, his face grimly set, fighting back the horror of the decision. "I'm going to have to take his leg. I don't really know a lot — I'm just a medic, but it's clear that if I don't, gangrene will set in. I'm going to have to take it. Shit." Bill stopped, swallowing hard as the agony of the situation overwhelmed him.

"I'm using... something that looks like a... small handsaw... to begin to cut through the bone. The sound of his shrieks sends chills throughout my entire body. I can feel the grind of the blade on bone! But I dare not stop — I just... keep... sawing..."

This is not what I had expected to hear. I found myself breathing deeply to make sure that I stayed with him —- present, alert, and listening with an open heart. This was, after all, a counseling session. But it was certainly unlike any other session that I'd ever done before in my 20-plus years as a therapist.

Bill (his name and some details changed to preserve confidentiality) had come to me, the vice-president of a successful company. He thought that somehow, he should be happy, but his life felt empty, as though nothing he did meant anything. He was clinically depressed.

I present workshops and lecture internationally. Often, when I am on the road, I stay in town for a few days and offer individual three-hour intensive sessions to try and create breakthroughs in relatively short periods of time. My book, The Quickening: Leaping Ahead on your Spiritual Journey was widely anticipated and initially sold out in three months. The Quickening describes how using cutting-edge modalities could accelerate the course of therapy and personal growth, sometimes through a single, powerful, life-changing experience. Often, readers would book an intensive with high expectations about what we could accomplish in three hours.

But, as Bill told his chilling story, I had sincere doubts about whether I was up to the task.

I knew that he was an experiencing a kind of a mid-life awakening. Bill was disappointed in his life and explained that mere financial success alone left him feeling like "I have a hole in my soul."

We do not need to have a near-death experience to have a so-called "life review" and see our life "flash before our eyes." Bill had consciously taken stock of his life and found it wanting.

As I knew more, I suggested that we use a technique called Brainspotting to help him re-evaluate his experience in a new light and to see if he couldn't find some direction toward the kind of life that he would be proud to call his own. Brainspotting is very good at rapidly changing core cognitions — deeply held, long term beliefs — in a short period of time.

Bill had said that he felt like his life was a failure, so I asked him to focus on that belief as we engaged the brainspotting process, which uses fixed eye positions and body-centered kinesthetic protocols to process trauma and shift negative beliefs. Brainspotting does not induce a trance but rather a very different way of processing information than we would do in a normal waking state.

But as Bill deeply mulled over his sense of lack of accomplishment and failure as a human being, his mind took a left turn didn't neither he nor I had anticipated.

He found himself in a past life!

In a vivid internal vision, he suddenly discovered himself on a bloody battlefield, experiencing life as a medic in the Civil War! Here were dozens of bodies lying around — some of them shrieking, a few moaning quietly, while others remained ominously still and silent.

"There's so many of them! I'm not a doctor! I'm just a medic! What do I know? How am I going to help anyone?" he cried out in desperation.

Instinctively, he found himself going to the man with a wounded leg. Despite his overwhelming sense of self-doubt, he somehow crudely amputated and bandaged it. He rushed to another wounded soldier - but this one was beyond help.

"Doc," the soldier said hoarsely, "am I going to be okay?" "I'm here," said Bill, grasping his hand, as well as the hopelessness of the situation. He looked deeply into the private's tear-filled eyes. "I'm here," Bill repeated, knowing he had not the courage to answer the question directly.

Instinctively, he began to say the Lord's prayer, barely above a whisper. The boy mumbled in unison. "... For thine is the kingdom, and the power, and the glory, forever, and ever. Amen," he intoned quietly. Opening his eyes, he looked down to see his patient, still and motionless. Bill paused for what seems like an eternity.

Then, he suddenly he burst into tears.

"I hate war! I HATE this! This is all so senseless! People dying for no reason! And there's nothing I can do! Am I just here to cut off legs? AM I JUST HERE TO HOLD SOMEONE'S HAND... ONLY TO SEE THEM DIE? I'M FUCKING USELESS!" he screamed.

Bill wept softly for several minutes. Then he was still.

"Why do we come to this goddamn planet? What difference can I possibly make?" muttered Bill, grimly. This was no time for some pithy psychobabble. I could only offer compassion.

"Dear God, Bill,' I said my voice cracking. "How horrible for you. How incredibly sad you were, trying the best you could and yet feeling so helpless and worthless. I'm so very sorry..."

Then Bill began weeping for all that he couldn't do in that life...and his current life. Minutes passed but then, though his eyes were closed, I could see he was looking at something in his mind's eye. "Somehow I can see the spirits of the men lifting up from their bodies...they are going upward." He gasped. "Oh God, they are all dead. I couldn't save them!" he said, filled with guilt and dread.

Nothing in my education prepared me for what to do next. I breathed into the stillness. And to my relief, a still small voice within me seem to offer direction. "Why don't you rise up with him and find those two soldiers? Talk to them. Tell them how you feel."

Sure enough, Bill saw himself rising up, too. He found the young men present that had died.

"I'm so very sorry...I tried... maybe if I knew more..." he trailed off. "Please... forgive me..." he said breathlessly. "I failed you." There was a pause and then Bill's face suddenly morphed into a look of puzzlement.

"He says that he forgives me, but that I didn't fail him! In fact, he is saying it over and over. I don't understand!"

Bill's brow furrowed. "He says that made all the difference because I was there when he died. And that as I prayed, he opened his heart and his soul to heaven...thy will be done, thy Kingdom come ...so that he could be released; released from the agony of war, released from the awful pain, released from his body!" He is saying, 'I knew you couldn't save my life. But the touch of your hand saved my soul!'"

Both of us found ourselves overwhelmed again, but this time with a very different kind of tears. The young soldier embraced Bill firmly, and then stepped back.

"See?" he said with a gentle expression, spreading his hands. "I'm whole again! You know...they really can't kill you," he commented to Bill with a quirky smile.

"Maybe... maybe I did make a difference..." Bill remarked, mulling the enormity of the moment. Then, his eyelids gently closed, as he took another easy breath.

"Here's another one, glowing in the distance!"

Bill somehow floated towards this energy, but suddenly grimaced as his body suddenly wrenched in agony. "Oh no, it's him! I cut his leg off while he screamed! What kind of monster am I? Why couldn't I save his leg? I tried, I swear to God, I tried..."

The young amputee grabbed Bill by both his shoulders.

"'You did the right thing! You saved my life!'"

"What?" said Bill "'You saved me! Really! The wound healed! The doc said you actually did a pretty good job — for a medic!'" He chuckled, as Bill stared at him in shock, wondering how he could possibly find that funny.

"See, because of you, my life was saved! I went back to my family farm and to my wife. You would have been proud of me! I got around pretty good on crutches — and sometimes a crappy wooden leg. I lived to a ripe old age! I had three children! I managed the farm with the help of others and my pension. I had a good life," he said, smiling broadly. Then his expression changed to mock seriousness. '"And yes, of course it hurt like hell when you cut off my leg, you son-of-a-bitch, you've got to find a better way to do that!'"

All three of us found ourselves laughing and crying at the same time.

Then, Bill felt the essence leave his presence and discovered himself lifting upward into a beautiful, radiant Light that completely enfolded him.

"Maybe, just maybe," I counseled Bill, "we are all just doing the best that we can. We have such high expectations of ourselves that we miss the little things that we do for people... that we don't really see how much our love matters to everyone around us."

"Yes," said Bill. "Not only in the intense moments, but in the simple everyday things: smiling at a neighbor, a hand on someone's shoulder, a phone call to someone who is lonely! You know, if we really got that, I think we would do a lot more of it."

For several minutes, somehow, I felt as though I, too, was being bathed in the presence of a Great Love that Bill was receiving more directly. Bill opened his eyes, his face filled with relief. Suddenly, he got an impish grin.

"Hey Gregg," he said, sounding like a naughty teenager hatching a prank, "I want to know if this guy really existed or I just made him up. Can you help me find out?" "Sure," I said responding confidently, not the least bit sure of myself. In fact, that I knew it was nigh on impossible, and yet, Bill's faith in me was so great, that I agreed.

"Bill," I said commandingly, "close your eyes and take a deep breath... "Taking him into a deeper trance state, I suggested that Bill go to the place where he was buried at the end of that life...

"I can see it..." he said excitedly. "I can really see it! I can read the name on the tombstone and the date of death! And I actually lived a couple more decades after the war! Wow!"

Those who are familiar with remote viewing or psychic experience will often say how difficult it is to get specific names and numbers. Consequently, I was delighted and amazed to see how quickly and easily Bill had picked them off.

"I get it now, Gregg," he said opening his eyes and looking at me with an unstoppable grin. "I've always made a difference. All of us do."

The shift I saw in Bill was truly wondrous. The profound spiritual teaching, A Course in Miracles, reminds us that "miracles collapse time." We had "re-wired" Bill's brain in just three hours. Bill had experienced an intense "shift in perception." A quickening!

We embraced warmly and I wished him well. Exhausted, I fell into an overstuffed easy chair in my suite.

POSTSCRIPT: Two months later, my cell phone rang. It was Bill and he was beyond excited. Although Bill's session was not intended to be a past life regression, but because I was certified as a regression therapist, having trained directly under Dr. Brian Weiss, author of the best-selling Many Lives, Many Masters, I could help Bill navigate those painful memories. But I also knew how uncommon it was for someone to find specific, undeniable evidence to support a past life memory.

So, what came next, was simply astonishing.

"Gregg, you won't believe this. I found the grave! I went there in person! The headstone looked a little different than in my vision, but the dates and the name were there! It's almost like 'proof' that it all really happened!" "Congratulations, Bill!" I exclaimed excitedly. But it wasn't until the next day, that I remembered something that Bill said in that phone call, that particularly struck me, causing me to tear up.

"I can't believe it!" he had said repeatedly. "There was my name on the headstone! I found myself! I found myself!

Indeed, he had.

Gregg Unterberger, M.Ed, is former adjunct faculty in Psychology at Texas State University, who currently lectures internationally and works as a licensed professional counselor in private practice, seeing clients across the country through encrypted tele-therapy online. He is the developer of two radical healing modalities, *Transpersonal Breathwork* and *Spiritual Activation,* which make powerful visionary states of consciousness available to virtually anyone. His book, *The Quickening: Leaping Ahead on Your Spiritual Journey* is approaching its fourth printing. His new book of poetry, *It Was You: Musings on Life, Love, Loss, and Why Children Feel the Need to Run Headlong into Your Groin at Disneyland,* and his new app, the WOKE a WORLDWIDE 8-WEEK CHALLENGE will be released in Spring of 2021.

When he is not counseling, you can usually find him laughing. Contact him on Facebook or at www.GreggUnterberger.com

BEYOND THE EXPLOSION

By Genny Krackau

When you are nine years of age, life is really quite simple and filled with few worries or concerns. Your main obligation is to help out at home, get along with your siblings and to make good grades at school. You enjoy sleep-overs with your friends, and you are delightfully excited when your Mom is taking out those fresh baked chocolate chip cookies from the oven. Life is good.

This was how it was in my young life, until one evening, when I was awakened in the middle of the night. As I laid in bed looking up at the ceiling, or what was once the ceiling, I had a clear view of many stars, planets and galaxies.

Even though I was laying on my back looking straight up, I could still clearly see everything in my room. I could see my sister sleeping, and wondering why she was not awake and experiencing this wonder. I felt I had many eyes and could see everything at once. I have since learned that this is called expanded vision... the all seeing eye of God.

And then, to the upper right of my vision, I saw who I thought was Jesus, smiling lovingly at me. He appeared to be enjoying my excitement of this spiritually transformative experience. He spoke to me and told me I had been given many gifts, powers and abilities and that I would be using them my entire life. He said I was a special child of God.

After this experience, I was confused and did not know who to talk with about what I had experienced. Since I attended Catholic school, I decided during recess I would go to the rectory to speak with a priest. Surely, a priest would understand what I had just experienced and would provide understanding and loving guidance. As I talked with the priest and attempted to explain my vision and seeing Jesus, he quickly dismissed me and told me to stop making up stories. It was obvious he thought I was making this all up when he told me to go back to recess. I left feeling so humiliated and never discussed this with anyone until my book, "Beyond the Explosion, Stories of the Light" was published in 2018.

Throughout my life, I continue to have Spiritually Transformative and Out of Body experiences. They all seem quite natural to me. I also receive heavenly messages, normally around 3 or 3:30 in the morning. I have learned to listen attentively to the messages. In 2013, I was awakened around 3 a.m. and the voice of God told me I was to write a book about combat near-death experiences. I mentally said, OK and attempted to go back to sleep when the voice told me "wait, the title of your book will be "Beyond the Explosion."

I had no idea the challenges and obstacles I would face to compile these stories. I knew little to nothing about near-death experiences. My Dad had a near-death experience during an operative procedure. This happened about three months before he passed of a massive heart attack. He shared his experience with me, but begged me not to discuss it with anyone as he felt no one would believe him.

I constantly prayed for guidance that Spirit would guide me in every way while I worked on my book. During my research, I quickly learned that experiencers were willing to share their stories but were not willing to put their stories in writing. This was very frustrating for me because their stories were amazing and should be shared.

It was fortunate that I spent my civil service career working in the U.S. Army Medical Department and retired from the U.S. Army Medical Command. Since my retirement I worked numerous government contract jobs and IN clinical research. Of special interest was a research study with wounded warriors who had combat related injuries, with the additional research of military and civilian burn injuries. Also, the hearing conservation research with the Department of Defense Hearing Center of Excellence. It was no surprise by compiling the combat near-death experience stories, that I was once again serving the military in a special and unique way.

I can totally relate to experiencers when they tell me their near-death, spiritually transformative, and out of body experiences are difficult to discuss fearing that no one will believe them. Our military sacrifice their lives for us and experience the unimaginable in combat as they describe in detail their war experience including the near-death, spiritually transformative, and out of body experiences (some had all three). Every story is unique and personal.

Divine guidance led me to compose this book of combat near-death experience stories to share with others in their quest of their own spiritual and Earthly journey.

My book "Beyond the Explosion, Stories of the Light" is available through Amazon.

Genny Krackau San Antonio, Texas.

Genny is a multiple STEr and OBEr. She is a member of the International Association of Near-Death Studies (IANDS). She has support the IANDS conferences as a volunteer, Co-facilitator of the IANDS Military NDE Workshop, Experiencer's Lounge and as a Panelist for the Military NDE Discussion Groups. She spent her Civil Service career working in the U.S. Army Medical Department (AMEDD) and retired from the U.S. Army Medical Command, Fort Sam Houston, Texas. Since her retirement, she worked several government contract jobs within the AMEDD. Of special interest was a research study with wounded warriors with combat related injuries. Additional research included military and civilian burn injuries, supporting a clinical trial for head injury patients, and hearing conservation research studies with the Department of Defense Hearing Center of Excellence. She is currently employed as a Research Associate for clinical trials in emergency trauma at a large university hospital in San Antonio.

She may be reached at www.lightstories.org or gkrackau@gmail.com.

DISBELIEF OF NDES

Leads to a "Medical & Spiritual Gap of Care" for Combat Soldiers.

By Lilia Samoilo

An injured soldier, having just had a Near-Death Experience (NDE), awakens in the hospital, confused and very emotional about an experience they do not understand. They may be traumatized from bodily injuries and in pain. They recall vivid memories of their life-changing NDE event and need answers to their many questions, seeking comfort and support. Reporting this to their medical provider, their questions are typically casually dismissed or go unanswered, leaving them with the impression to not discuss their NDE further and left in an emotional limbo.

They may become fearful that they will not be believed, or that they will be rejected, ridiculed, mischaracterized as "mental" or misdiagnosed as psychotic and treated with unwarranted drug therapies, which can produce serious side effects. In addition, they may worry that discussing their NDE might make them at risk to lose their security clearance and benefits.

Wounded soldiers, feeling vulnerable, place their trust in the medical staff and clergy to care, comfort and support them regarding their life-altering NDE. Unfortunately, more times than not, their NDE account is dismissed or trivialized by the very medical personnel sworn to heal them. Instead, they may be given sedatives or other drugs, to help cope with any perceived stress associated with their "so-called" NDE.

The first line of defense to assist patients who have had an NDE should take place at their bedside in the hospital, by medical personnel or clergy trained to deal with patients who have experienced an NDE. But that is just not the case, producing a patient "gap of care."

NDEs are not typically accepted as a "real" event among the medical community and clergy. They are oftentimes considered to be non-factual; an illusion produced by post-traumatic stress, or perhaps a lack of oxygen etc. The denial of the NDE being a "real" event leads to this "gap of care." This lack of validation of the NDE account can have a damaging impact on the soldier's psyche, causing them to lose confidence in expressing their NDE. They are left on their own to "work it out" and often revert to conditioned responses taught during combat training, suppressing their feelings deep inside, which complicates their PTSD.

The impact of this crucial "gap of care" should not be marginalized. It is not merely a missed opportunity to help resolve concerns the soldier may have about their NDE. The "gap of care" is traumatizing to the soldier, exacerbating an already devastating, life-changing injury, including PTSD, and magnifying feelings of confusion, fear, isolation and hopeless despair, with little to no way out.

NDEs are a real experience to the soldier and must be validated as such.

Lilia Samoilo, Neologist

"Do you want to see

beyond what you see?"

This question was asked of me within a lucid dream, and I gave enthusiastic answer of YES! to the light, and then I made an eternal promise to share all that I discovered.

Claudia Watts Edge

Chapter Three

EXAMINING TIME

Ken Root:	OUTSIDE OF TIME
Barbara Mango PhD:	TRANSENDING TIME
Larry Vorwerk:	VISITING A PARALLEL UNIVERSE OUTSIDE OF TIME

OUTSIDE OF TIME

The VW Bug Rollover

By Ken Root

I'm in my 60s now and remember my first NDE like it was yesterday. It was the early 1970s, I was 17, and had just graduated high school in an affluent suburb of Chicago. We had a house guest stay with us from Brazil over a previous summer and I had an open invitation to come visit his family. That summer I had the time and money to travel on my own for the first time in my life, so I took him up on his offer and traveled solo. I spent the entire summer in Brazil before starting my college years.

I had an incredible experience traveling all over Brazil and many neighboring countries. Most of the summer, however, was pretty boring hanging out at home base in the suburbs of Sao Paulo. I was off on summer break, but all the other kids my age there were still in school. Most of my days were spent sitting on the edge of a viewpoint looking down over Sao Paulo, waiting for my friends to get out of school so we can go have fun together.

In retrospect, I had no real understanding what meditation was but that's exactly what I was doing. Absolutely nothing. I also did not speak Portuguese but by the end of the summer I was getting pretty fluent and was dreaming in it. I was no longer thinking in English, or words at all for that matter. My brain was going through a neural network of reprogramming as I learned a new language like a baby does... By immersion and listening. I met very few people to speak English with for months. My old identity had been left behind in the USA with my family.

On weekends, we'd load up insanely overpowered go-carts and head to Interlagos International Speedway where we'd hit speeds well over 100mph in the straights. On school days, however, our normal routine began when my friends would get home and we'd pile into VW Beetles to practice our racing techniques on the streets of Sao Paolo. Confronting danger and fear was part of the machismo fun and thrill of it.

One day, for no logical reason I felt irrationally uncomfortable getting into the car. I knew not to get in, and clearly told my friends that I didn't want to go with them that day. After being teased, insulted, and called diminishing names, I reluctantly got in the car and we tore off into our usual routine of taking turns practicing high speed drifting.

That particular day I could not control my fear like I normally was able to. It was "Fear" unshackled. I could feel my adrenaline increasing moment by moment and nothing I could do would affect it. I thought perhaps putting on my seat belt might help me better control my rising fear, so despite knowingly humiliating myself for being a coward, I reached down and buckled the belt.

The best way I can describe that seat belt click is to imagine a gigantic, sweaty sumo wrestler swinging a Thor sized hammer into an enormous gong. I'd never before experienced that sort of Earth quaking, internal "resonance" before, (Since that moment I have learned to stop and listen VERY carefully to it. It's warned me of danger repeatedly since.) That buckle-click non-verbally and instantly validated what was coming. (In retrospect, it was a download, but my mind didn't understand yet.) In the instant of that click my body knew what was coming and took over as my mind passively observed... feeling totally clueless as my hands quickly prepared me for the accident.

I was sitting in the right rear passenger seat, and without any conscious thought or planning, I quickly unbuckled the belt, and removed the green, woolen lumberjack coat I had on. I then buckled both the lap and shoulder belts. The loud mocking and laughing at my cowardice from my friends seemed like they were miles away in the distance... I barely noticed them and no longer cared. Have you ever listened to a bottle filling with water and guessed without looking when it's going to overflow by focusing on the sound? That's what I experienced, but with fear instead of sound. I could feel a life changing moment in time approaching and could tell how much time I had left by the energy charge building within me, and for some reason, I tightly wrapped the coat around my right arm. I braced my right palm against the front of the side window frame, pushing myself back into the seat, leaving the coat tail hanging down and covering the bottom of the window. With my left hand I reached under my seat and grabbed the seat frame and pulled myself down into the seat. I then took a big deep breath and counted down 3-2-1 and on zero I looked over the edge of my coat as the street came up to the window at the exact millisecond I knew it would. I closed my eyes, and we began a triple rollover into busy traffic.

At the precise instant, the window next to me exploded, time stopped, and my fear vanished. There was only complete stillness. My first thought was "What's happening to me!!!," and I was immediately answered with the clear message that I was safe and protected. I could

feel the love. I can best describe these messages as thought packets...
an entire download of information in an instant without words or
language. In other words, if I say the English noun "book," you might
imagine briefly in your mind what a book looks like, and an internal
symbol in your mind for what a book means to you. In another
language, perhaps Portuguese, if I say "livro" and you imagine a book,
you get to the same conceptual model regardless of language, right? For
lack of a better term, I call it symbolic understanding. These
communications were sent directly to what's behind the auditory
processing centers of the senses. Instantaneous bursts of
understanding, as clear and real as any physical conversation, in fact.
probably more-clear since misinterpreting spoken words wasn't
possible.

At first, I thought time had completely stopped, but then (with
eyes tightly closed) when I carefully listened to the glass tinkling by
around me, I could tell time was indeed moving, but incredibly slow.
The exploding window particles moved around me like thousands of
snails barely moving in every possible direction. What caught my
attention was how the tinkling sounds they made sounded perfectly
normal, which made no sense at all because if you slow down an audio
recording the pitch of the sound changes, but that was not happening
in this case. Listening to the chaos around me while suspended in time,
my mind was completely absorbed in: 1) who is answering my
questions? 2) what happened to my fear? 3) how can time be slowed
and sounds unaffected? 4) am I going to die? At that point I think my
mind totally gave up the steering wheel of control and stepped aside to
go ponder those questions while something new opened up in me.

With eyes still closed I could "see" the glass particles in my
mind's eye. My first thought was that it was like echo-location that bats
do, that I was forming a 3D view in my mind of the space around me
based on the sounds of colliding glass particles suspended in the air
around me. I soon discovered I could focus on an individual particle of

glass going by, and "look" at it from any distance or angle around it. This did not make sense.

As I was remote viewing the particles, I wondered what the outcome of this accident was going to be and if I was going to be ok. My point of view unexpectedly went upward straight through the metal roof of the car and similar to how I could "see" the glass particles, I could view the accident from outside the car. After a brief pause, as if to answer my concern, a "ghost image" of the car fast forwarded in time. I watched it roll from any viewpoint I wanted and watched as it rolled three times and landed on all four wheels. I felt a sigh of relief, and like a pop, I was instantly back in my body near the very beginning of the accident. I thought it was kind of cool and did this several times to assure myself I was going to be ok. I could freely go back to my body and listen to the chaos with my eyes closed from there, or it was MUCH more interesting to go exploring in my mind's eye from 3D and 4D (time) perspectives.

Here's my best description of the experience and how the navigation controls worked.

I knew I was a locus point of observation, an infinitely small, 360 degree camera view. Navigation was based on intent, not thought. If we're in deep meditation, totally present, and without thought, we can still open and close our eyes, right? It was like that. Before I could even try to form a thought, the answer would arrive. When I was navigating through time, colors and solid form would be left behind and it was like putting on the ring of power in Lord of the Rings where things turn to smoky, shifting, semi-transparent grayscale. When I'd slow down in the time stream and focus on specific objects, colors would return, even in displaced time. And I had the sense of time being more like a 3D venetian blind than a linear movie film strip. In other words, imagine stacking flat plates together with space between them. Now imagine an infinite number of them forming a stream like a long ribbon floating in weightless space. In addition to being able to move my viewpoint anywhere in 3D space around the accident, if I moved between the slats, time would move forward and backwards like a VCR control. I could also move outside the slats and see the time stream from above. Like a dolphin breaching and diving, I could pop out, look around the blackness of space (not very interesting), and dive back into the stream. Each slat in the stack when viewed from inside was a 3D moment of now. From outside, the slats were 2D cross sections of the stream.

I was so fascinated exploring time, it never occurred to me to ask more questions to my host/guide. All I can describe is it was a warm, loving, and perhaps male presence. I say perhaps because I didn't see him and only have memories of how his communications felt. If I handed you a wood block of light, soft pine and a block of dark, hard walnut, and asked you which is male... the denser wood seems like a good guess, right? It felt like that so the gender is an intuitive guess.

I remember when we finally got around to the 3rd roll of the vehicle that after the two previous rolls, it was starting to get old and I just settled into waiting to get it over with. I was in complete and total disbelief that we had enough momentum to finish the final roll as I had watched it repeatedly play out in advance. We were obviously moving too slow. It seemed like a ball impossibly rolling uphill on its own. We teetered on two wheels for a long time. The final drop onto all four wheels seemed to take forever, followed by a big bounce on the shocks as we landed upright. The instant we landed, immediately my guide quite loudly insisted that I first take off my glasses and gently brush the powdered glass from my eye lids. I did slowly, before opening my eyes and looking around.

The driver's side door on the left side was wide open and the driver's seat was unlatched in the forward position against the steering wheel. It felt very weird, like valet service inviting me to step out of the car while they hold the door handle for me. Next to me in the back seat my friend was unconscious with a concussion. As I stepped out of the vehicle I noticed another friend with his upper torso through the windshield, unconscious. I didn't see the driver anywhere (I learned the next day at the hospital he was thrown out the door and shattered his collar bone and ribs.)

Assuming it was over and wanting to get to safety, I stepped out into the sunlight in the middle of the street. It was a busy multi-lane roundabout with a fountain in the middle, shops all around, and traffic was panic-stopped all around us. People started pouring out of the shops to see the accident. It was then that I realized I was still impacted by the event. I found that I could "see" through the eyes of everyone around me. I looked at a group of male teens and could see their glee "Nascar! Stock cars! More!" When a warm, caring, elderly woman stepped out of one of the shops, I could see the association she was having with a serious car accident her son recently had. I could see his bearded face and feel her love for him. I wondered what his name was, but couldn't quite reach out and touch it.

I think that must have been the last straw for my mind. That woman was my last memory of this event. It was like a switch got flipped and everything after that was erased. I was in a foreign country; my friends were unconscious and heading to the ER without me. I had no familiarity with the streets, no map, didn't speak the language, and cell phones weren't invented yet. I was completely lost... and yet the next day I remember waking up at the family's house hosting me as I normally did and was driven that morning to visit my friends in the hospital. I have always wondered how I found my way back to where I was staying. A psychic friend once told me she intuits that my guides led me home. I don't know. With no frame of reference on NDEs, none of this made any sense to me.

The next day my friends were three beds in a row with ropes, pulleys, and lots of plaster casts. What we all immediately noticed was that I did not have a single scratch or the slightest nick, Anywhere. They had me roll up my sleeves in disbelief. They looked like they had been blasted at close range with a shotgun. Hands, arms, faces, even their hair and scalps... There was not a single square inch of exposed skin that didn't have cuts, most of which were right angle nicks from the squares of exploding glass. My mind rationalizes my not getting a scratch by the fact that I was completely strapped in and wasn't rolling around in the car like they did. What I don't understand, is I don't think anything touched me. I never felt a piece of glass bounce off or the friend next to me being tossed around the car.

While I was bedside at the hospital, we made a pact to never tell anyone "the American" was in the car. It was a secret to all family, police, insurance, etc. I didn't tell anyone. In fact, I was so terrified and traumatized by the entire experience I never wanted to think about it ever again. I totally believed I had a stress induced nervous breakdown and moved on with my life.

Part 2: Motorcycle collision (but not mine!)

A few years later I was home for the summer from college and went to a A few years later I was home for the summer from college and went to a city park to party and hang out with friends. A loud chopper-style Harley motorcycle with long forks and handlebars drove through the park and I was astonished by the exact same feeling I experienced in the click of the seat belt in the VW Beetle rollover. It made absolutely no sense but out of the blue, this guy was ringing that familiar bell. Loud! I turned to my friend and said "Watch this guy... I think he's going to have an accident." We then watched the biker leave the park and drive off into the distance.

I slowly nursed my beer and went deep in thought. It was like my intuition had betrayed me. I felt confused and was just trying to figure out what that feeling might have possibly meant. All I knew is the feeling I had was real and powerful.

Perhaps an hour later I was suddenly made aware that I was walking away from the picnic table where my friends were sitting when

I heard the words behind me "Hey, where are you going?" I wanted to say, "I don't know!" but I couldn't respond. I didn't know why I was walking or where to, but my body was in motion. I walked a few hundred feet to the side of the main road through the park and stopped. I "knew" these are the time/space coordinates I was meant to be at and immediately as I stepped on that spot I could feel the vibration of that motorcycle approaching in my mind's eye before I could hear it with my ears. Soon I could hear the distant thunder of the Harley's engine and my mind was skeptically going, "yea, right!" Then he turned into the park and it was definitely the same biker but this time he had a woman riding on the back seat.

Coming out of the park at the same time from the other direction was a big, athletic looking guy on a 750 Honda. As they converged, it became apparent to me that they would cross each other directly in front of me. As they approached, the chopper dude coming from my right raised his arm to wave to friends in the park to his right and shifted his weight to his left. His bike crossed over the middle, and both handlebars collided directly in front of me. I was standing on grass at the curb, literally arm's reach away. At the precise instant, the handlebars clicked, time stopped.

My first thought was "WTF! NOT AGAIN!!!!!" I was so sure the VW rollover NDE was my imagination. The exact same presence as last time replied, "You tried to stuff it last time and so it had to happen to you again." (That's the closest I can come to an exact quote. It was very clear.) I was once again able to explore time and space. There was definitely less fear this time because I knew I was in no danger, so I was a bit more relaxed and inquisitive than my first NDE. I rode motorcycles for many years and a flash of concern hit me for the safety of the girl on the back seat. She probably doesn't even know yet what's happening and will be most at risk of serious injury. I watched her ghost image roll forward out of her body from the bike, she tried to land on her feet, but when her tennis shoes hit the pavement she started to roll. As her knee touched down on the initial contact with the asphalt, my point of view leaped forward to within inches of her knee in full color high def. I vividly remember watching her knee roll on the pavement and could inspect every detail of the minor scrape she was about to receive. With my concern resolved, the accident snapped back to near the beginning again. I seriously wondered if I could help her, but I would have needed to step in front of the 750 Honda and wasn't confident how real world physics would treat me in this state. I decided a minor scrape of the knee wasn't worth the safety risk to my body and relaxed to soak it all in.

What I was told very clearly by my guide is this was happening for my benefit and my benefit alone... don't try to convince your friend or anyone else. Since I had spoken the prediction around an hour earlier, I insisted to my guide that I had proof and my friend would believe me. (My friend's exact words later were "You and your ESP are full of sh*t.") My friend wasn't spiritual at all and I wasn't too surprised by his response, but I'll always remember being talked down to with patience and love by the guide. Like a child that lives in a small apartment demanding a real pony, I'd insist my prediction was proof and I'd get back a kind and calm "Nope, this is just for you. Pay attention."

I was given the parting message that it was critical that I remember these experiences for the rest of my life... and we'll talk again later in this life. It was vague what that meant as far as time, and I wondered if it would be my death bed. That message seemed deliberately vague and open ended. Free will, I assume.

Summary of parts 1 and 2:

Part 1 seems to fit the traditional NDE patterns I've read about. I truly believed I was going to die in the rollover accident and was in extreme fear and emotional duress. In part two with the bikes, I was never in danger and knew I was perfectly safe the entire time. Yet they were so similar. Like yin and yang.

The only emotional duress I was under during the bike accident was confusion over what seemed like a false prophesy, (until it wasn't anymore.) Clearly, Round 1 was an NDE. Round 2 seemed somehow different than many NDE stories I've read. Both were divine intervention, but the second time was not to save my life, but to give me an important message that these experiences are quite real. Spirit had to get out a longer 2x4 to get me to pay attention the second time.

I'm stubborn, rational, and scientific. I've been a computer engineer most of my working life. If either of these experiences had occurred in isolation I wouldn't have believed either. In retrospect, it really did take both of these events together to blast through my denial. Without any understanding of what happened to me and no frame of reference or support systems, I focused on career and family for the next 40 years or so and tried not to think about my NDEs. I told very few people. Many of the friends I did share stories with would quickly exit my life. (Especially evangelical friends that would ask me my thoughts about God. Ouch!) My son was an adult before I shared these stories with him. My wife had to nudge me at the dinner table not very long ago to finally tell him.

HeartMath:

I could end this tale here, but it would be incomplete without my personal HeartMath shout-out. Fast forward 40 or 50 years to just a few years ago. I was working for a large, well known Silicon Valley company. I'm in my 60s and working with some of the most brilliant and competitive young engineers on the planet. I had never heard of the "dark night of the soul," but I lived it when I was targeted by an extreme narcissist at work that went on a vicious campaign to destroy me for refusing to be his obedient minion. I started having blinding optical migraines and PTSD symptoms, triggered by stress coming from multiple directions at once. I was put on a low dose beta blocker to reduce my adrenal response (which worked) but after a year or so, I tried to reduce the dosage and discovered it would trigger an attack within hours. I had to detox slowly and face up to better managing the stress in my life. I purchased a HeartMath EmWave2 portable biofeedback sensor to see if I could use it to improve my meditation practice and lower my heart rate under stress. It did, but that's beside the point of this story.

At first I found the gadget incredibly frustrating. It starts off with a red LED and when you're able to calm your pulse, breath, and relax, it will shift to blue and make a beeping sound every 10 seconds or so. That's called "medium coherence." If you can fill yourself with positive thoughts such as gratitude, puppies, your "happy place," etc. it will shift to a green LED and beep a happier tone. It drove me nuts at first because it requires the opposite of effort. As soon as it would blink into green, I'd think "I got this" and instantly it would flatline to red. The instant I'd give up and reach the put it away... blue. As if it was taunting me. Clearly, it took me a while to figure out "Don't push the river." (It does get easier with practice!)

Very early after I purchased the gadget and was getting annoyed by how difficult it seemed, the weird thought occurred to me, what if I imagine being in the trauma of the VW beetle NDE? Would it go red instantly? My jaw dropped in dumbfounded astonishment when I discovered it was the most powerful way I could find to achieve full coherence in seconds. Instead of struggling for 15 minutes to occasionally see results, it would skip past blue right into green, bleep, bleep, done. SAY WHAT? How could an event that carried so much fear, that talking about makes my heart race, possibly fast track me into coherence? It was measurable and repeatable. Life was giving me a Zen koan to ponder, investigate, and unlock.

What I learned from the HeartMath EmWave2 is that my body knew the truth and the gadget... a piece of hardware containing a sensor, CPU, battery, and some firmware algorithms, is only capable of reading what my heartbeat is telling it. It was challenging me to re-examine if my NDEs were really the trauma I believed. Were they really something to fear and avoid?

With practice and trial and error the following imagery has become something I still try to incorporate into my meditation practice using HeartMath. Imagine being strapped into the back seat of that easy to roll (like a beachball), VW beetle. A vehicle somewhat optimized for this accident by its round shape. Now imagine that instead of you being tossed around, the entire event is swirling around you. Imagine being the epicenter of the vortex, the calm, and still eye at the center of the tornado. Chaos and destruction all around, while you are invisibly being caressed around the shoulders from behind, wrapped in the indestructible, loving wings of an angel. From that point of view, it doesn't sound like trauma, does it? The HeartMath gadget was reading the love I received and was still trying to deny, not the fear I still imagined and clung to. My point is this has been the essence of the "Hero's Journey" for me... how past trauma can be realized as a blessing if you examine it more carefully. The electronic gadget called my BS and was a catalyst that helped unlock a deeper understanding of my NDEs and the fear I held around them most of my life.

Epilogue:

The universe knocked on my door as a young man and I lacked the maturity, wisdom, and support systems to say yes to the invitation. While I could no longer deny what happened to me after my 2nd experience, I kept them a closely guarded secret most of my life. It took me almost 50 years to integrate these explosive awakenings and be able to more openly talk about them. For other experiencers that are afraid of what people will think, I encourage you to be your authentic self and talk about your experiences. It's quite liberating to consciously step beyond fear, and I believe it also benefits receptive listeners.

I see many Facebook posts from non-experiencers expressing envy for those that have had NDEs. I quite seriously would never wish what happened to me on anyone. It's like randomly getting struck by lightning and waking up in the hospital afterwards trying to understand and adapt to the unwanted and unexpected intrusion to your life. For me, I found it's something to recover from, not something to envy or seek. I'm beginning to understand that the mind is linear, and spirit is multidimensional. Mind can't begin to understand the other side and blindly seeks external answers that don't exist in this world of form. The best you can do is integrate experiences like these through inquiry and seeking a larger perspective. With free will we can see NDEs as trauma, or we can choose to dig deeper to see that they are often also a huge blessing in disguise. Getting to that realization can be a long and difficult road but it's quite possible and highly rewarding to do so.

What did I learn most from my NDEs? That we are awareness itself, a locus point of observation. That I am loved and protected. That my support network is MUCH wider and deeper than our senses can perceive. That what an experiencer needs to hear most from others is the indisputable fact that nobody can deny that what you experience within you is real for you and nobody else's opinion matters. This life is precious and has a freshness date. Don't run away from the calling, investigate it for yourself.

When I recently started "coming out" by sharing these NDE stories, a frequent question has been if these experiences completely eliminated my fear of death. Honestly, no. Lessened perhaps but not eliminated as completely as I hear from so many experiencer stories. I think it's because I realize how precious life is and how little time we have here.

Ken Root, US Pacific Northwest

Ken went into respiratory failure on the operating table due to a skull fracture at age 3 and is a childhood NDE experiencer. When the microprocessor was first invented, he taught himself how to program computers at a chip level and rode the high-tech wave from room sized mainframes computers to modern day mobile devices over a long and successful career. Now retired in the US Pacific Northwest, he's an active member of the NDE community and is the administrator for Lee Witting's NDE Radio show on Youtube. Ken can be reached at iamkroot1@gmail.com

Photo by Mike Schultz *www.uv21* is used by permission

My Brother Jeff and I

I have two vivid memories as a kid growing up in the 1950's and 60's and the worldly advances and technological wonders. The first came after excusing myself from the dinner table, and turning the dial on the TV to find a program called the Flintstones. It was playing in the evening, unheard of in those days of three channel choices of mostly news or variety shows. Cartoons were slated for 6 am on Saturdays, and kids were tuned to spring out of bed in time for a slew of animated choices between sets of commercials of toys and cereal ads.

I ran back to the kitchen with all of the excitement and joy a six-year-old could carry, screaming "CARTOONS AT NIGHT, CARTOONS AT NIGHT! My brother Jeff jumped away from his plate so fast his chair tipped backwards and hit the floor as he scrambled to get to the four-legged box, complete with the rabbit ears antenna on top. We glued our attention to the screen filled with the miracle of black and white drawings coming to life as a family from the stone ages that marked our own presence in the future...

The second wonder came in the form of a digital paneled clock in the early 60's. Jeff and I spent every Christmas Eve parked at the bottom of the basement stairs watching the numbers on the clock scroll by... ever so slowly... each second marked an important step towards making the minute dial begin it's scroll at an even slower crawl. We were diligent in our determination to stay awake and watch until the hour panel reached the glorious number 5, and the instructed time that Christmas could officially begin.

Jeff and I learned valuable lessons about time in those years together, finding that a watched clock moved very slowly, as opposed to how fast the kid years can fly by. Ken's story of standing outside of time, directing it, reviewing it, speeding it up and then slowing it down for closer examination is a remarkable example of time, or no time at all. Perhaps our lives here on earth are marked more by the events, than in an exact measure of time. The events able to be revisited, frozen still or flipped forward, as Ken was aware that 'something' was coming, like it had already happened.

In our Earth state of mind, it is hard to imagine 'no time' especially of its hold over each of our days and finding the lack of it as we set our watches and alarm clocks to the beat of the ticking clock. I have to admit I have a limited understanding of linear time and the talk of the lack of it, but I am fascinated by Kenneth's example of being able to see it, work with it, turn it over and upside down for a closer look. Just Fascinating stuff Ken, thank you.

TRANSCENDING TIME

By Barbara Mango PhD

From the time I was verbal, I knew I was different. What normal two-year old comprehends that other dimensions exist beyond space and time? How was I capable of understanding this at such a tender age? Regardless, I just knew, unequivocally, that Earth was not my "real" home, and merely a 3-D construct. I was always aware that I was an unusual child; different, unique, not quite fitting in. My mother once said to me, "If I didn't remember giving birth to you, I would never think you were mine. You are so different than the rest of us." I will never forget that comment. Throughout my childhood, I felt like an unloved and misunderstood "freak." As a result, I have spent the majority of my life struggling with self-esteem and a deep need to be loved and accepted unconditionally.

As a child, I was always daydreaming. My vivid imagination helped me escape from an abusive, unloving, and unhappy childhood. My parents used to tell me, "You live in your own world." My mother nicknamed me "Sarah Bernhardt" (a French stage actress active in the late 19th-20th century). Bernhardt was known for her over-the-top onstage gesturing and highly theatrical lifestyle. I was deeply offended by the nickname and my family's inability or unwillingness to take me seriously. In their view, I over-exaggerated and fantasized, and lacked the ability to live in the "real world." In actuality, I saw the reality of my childhood with crystal clarity. I just didn't happen to like it.

Instead of family, the natural world became my refuge, my place of solace, safety, and stillness. I was filled with the wonder of nature - the magnificent beauty of flowers, the gentle, yet majestic strength of trees, and the sweet smell of freshly cut grass. Nature, unlike my family, did not judge me. Instead, it offered me a world of exquisite beauty and respite. To this day, nature is my nirvana, my "go-to" place to decompress and ground myself. Taking a walk always restores my mind and soul.

Yet, one walk in particular forever changed me. It profoundly transformed my understanding of time and space, helped to heal my unloved inner child, and revealed the inexplicable magnificence of God/Source/All that is. I recorded this beatific experience in my journal immediately afterwards.

Journal Entry/Transcendent Walk

September 28, 2016

I am dumbfounded. Speechless. Overcome with intense emotions of enormous proportion, depth, and beauty. I just returned to my house after a walk down my street. It is a beautiful fall day outside - warmish, with a brilliant blue sky dotted with puffy white clouds. As I walked, I looked upwards. I felt unusually drawn to the sky. Halfway down the street I stopped walking - giving my full attention to the blueness above me-mesmerized. And then IT happened. Time ceased to exist, while, simultaneously, I was enveloped by a love 1000x more powerful than I have ever experienced on earth. Pure, unconditional love. I knew, without a doubt, that I was surrounded by and being embraced by Source. Human words are utterly inadequate to describe the intensity of such bliss. Love permeated every fiber of my being.

I was aware that I was standing on the pavement; that my feet were rooted to the road, that I was inhabiting my 3-D, human body. Yet, simultaneously, I was connected with ALL THAT IS, and time lost all meaning. It was if I were suspended in time.

I began receiving downloads of telepathic information from Source at warp speed, yet, I comprehended it immediately and fully. God was demonstrating to me the interconnection of not only every being, but everything on our earth and in our universe/multiple universes. From a single blade of grass to the world's highest peak; the intricate beauty of a spider's web, to a simple speck of dirt. I was overwhelmed with this profound knowledge, yet its comprehension was as natural as breathing.

While I continued to soak up this incredible information, Source began revealing to me the origin of the Universe and formation of all celestial objects. I instantaneously understood the math, physics, and science that astronomy is based on. In that instant, I thoroughly comprehended quantum mechanics and theoretical physics. In everyday life, however, I struggle to understand biology and barely grasp Algebra I. Yet, this exceedingly complex information was effortless to understand. It seemed so simple, so natural, a knowledge I had buried deep within my soul, yet remained unable to tap into in 3-D reality. I became one with the universe-feeling its love and magnetic pull envelope me.

I was shown delicate, thread-like stands of energy connecting every form of life. These radiant wisps were magnificent to behold-shimmering threads of golden-white light.

In that moment I realized two things-at our essence, everything in the Universe is interconnected by pure, energetic love, and additionally, humanity is unconditionally loved by Source. A love so deep, so pure, and so full, it cannot be described in limited human vocabulary. My heart was bursting. I was overwhelmed with emotion. Source's capacity for love is unfathomable to human beings-infinite souls trapped in temporary physical bodies.

Source continued imparting information to me wordlessly. "All of creation is interconnected, nothing stands alone. Know that you are dearly loved."

It no longer mattered that I had not received unconditional love as a child. I now understood that I was loved, cherished, and accepted by something infinitely greater than my family of origin.

At this point, my transcendent experience ended as suddenly as it began. I once again became fully aware of my surroundings-I was back rooted in reality. Tears of joy were running down my face, which was still turned upward-still looking towards the sky. The information download and immense knowledge that I had received immediately began fading. I retained only small pieces of this encounter. Yet, the only lesson I needed to carry forward in my physical life was my newfound comprehension of love.

Afterwards, I wondered how long this encounter had lasted. Five minutes? Thirty seconds? I had no idea. It just was, and then, it wasn't. Time itself, had lost all meaning.

In our everyday, 3-D reality, humanity is governed by time. We attempt to place it in neat and tidy compartments in order to define and organize our lives. Time is measured by schedules and meetings; clocks and calendars, lunar cycles, days, minutes, and hours, and the rising and setting of the sun. We categorize it by past (history), present (now), or future (the period after the present moment). The English language is filled with familiar phrases, further entrenching us in the illusion that time is "real." We are all familiar with catchphrases such as:

"Time stood still." "What time is it?" "It's time for lunch."

Thus, it is difficult, if not impossible, for most individuals to imagine a world in which time and space do not exist. Yet, other-worldly experiencers consistently describe time as a matrix, or alternate reality. One in which the past, present, and future exist simultaneously, or cease to exist at all.

My spontaneous past life memories center on earlier historical times and places. Meanwhile, my precognitive dreams focus on unknown, future events. Yet, in this experience, time, as we know it, was non-existent. The past, future, and present were one and the same.

Source demonstrated to me that the human energy body extends beyond space/time, connecting all with pure, unconditional love. This was a lesson, an event, a beauteous, and transformational experience. I will never be the same.

Barbara Mango, Ph.D.

Author of Convergence: The Interconnection of Extraordinary Experiences

Barbara Mango,Ph.D.

Twitter: @ExperiencerOm

Facebook: journeysintoconsciousness

http://www.extraordinaryexperiences.org

http://www.indiebound.org/book/9781636490549

VISITING A PARALLEL UNIVERSE

By Larry Vorwerk

2/27/2020

Before I get into my story, I would like to define some terms and give a little background to assist with understanding my experience. I think this will help you grasp the true experience.

"An out-of-body experience (OBE) is a phenomenon in which a person perceives the world from a location outside their physical body." The person's consciousness leaves the physical body and travels to another place and sometimes to another time. The physical sensations and level of consciousness is the same as in our physical world here on Earth that you and I are now living. It has been said that about one in ten people will have had at least one OBE in their lifetime.

"Parallel Universe in quantum mechanics is a universe theorized as existing alongside our own, although undetectable." Modern physicists now believe and theorize that our universe bumps up to other universes.

We are pure consciousness. Our physical body is just a covering we inhabit while living out our physical lives here on Earth. As such our consciousness lives on beyond this physical world. There are many levels of consciousness. Science will sometime describe them as dimensions of reality. While living out our lives on Earth, we are focused on one of the lower levels of our high self/God self-consciousness. As we evolve and grow, we continue to raise our level of consciousness where we can experience higher and higher levels of reality beyond this world.

We perceive time as linear while living in our physical bodies in our third dimensional world. Science believes there are at least eleven dimensions to reality. In the higher dimensions, time is not linear from the standpoint of going from the past to the future. Instead, present moment is the only time there is—or "No Time." This is a difficult concept to understand unless a person has had a Near-Death Experience (NDE) or a Spiritually Transformative Experience (STE) where everything exists and happens at the same time or in the Eternal Now.

Here is my experience that I want to share.

This morning I woke up from an OBE where I went to a parallel universe. I went back in time for thirty or more years; and in this parallel universe, most things were as they are here in this universe.

Here are some details and highlights taken from this experience.

In this other universe, my parents were still alive and looking healthy at about age sixty. They both passed away fifteen and seventeen years ago. In this other universe we were all living in the house where I grew up. Everything looked almost the same as it did in this universe. While there I realized my parents died many years ago, but they were alive in this reality. I acknowledged that and said to them, "it is so good to see you again." My parents and some of my siblings just laughed because in this universe they knew our parents were still alive. Being excited, I asked my dad If I could give him a hug. Of course he said yes, kind of a "why not" response. I realized something was different, so I asked what date it was? My sister looked confused when I asked that, so I looked on the wall for a calendar to see the date. It had different markings on the calendar, with nine days in a week. And yet, they didn't call them Sunday, Monday, etc. There were no years on the calendar, but there was some other type of acknowledgement to keep track of time.

I remember asking my sister for some paper so I could write this all down and take it back with me. She kept giving me paper with a lot of writing on it, so I kept asking for some clean paper. By the time I got some clean paper I woke up or came back to this universe. There was a lot more to the experience, but you get the idea. In any case it was so good to see my parents again, as they had been, and to give them a heart-felt hug. I realize this is an alternative way to see people whom you loved that have passed on over to the other side of the veil. I've had a few other alternative universe experiences before but not quite like this one. It was very emotional. For me, it brings up this question about alternate universes. Have we lived where things are mostly the same but with some things altered?

Giving this experience a little more thought, I realized I had an OBE where I traveled back into a parallel universe. It was very real, because I could be totally aware that I was literally hugging my dad. It brought tears to my eyes. I was about thirty years younger; and yet, at the same time, I realized I was actually sixty-eight years old in this universe. My brothers and sisters were not aware of my being from this other universe. It was so surreal and yet so wonderful at the same time.

This convinces me that we are so much more than just a body living in this time and space in this universe. We each truly are a consciousness that exist throughout time and space.

By Larry Vorwerk, Northfield Minnesota

Author of the Book: "The Bartholomew Effect: Awakening to Oneness"

Facebook Group:
http://www.facebook.com/groups/Awakening2Oneness/
Facebook Page: https://www.facebook.com/pages/Awakening-to-Oneness/194054543945963

"After coming back,

I fell in Love with all that there is,

From all that I had learned."

Alan R. Stevenson

Chapter Four

LIFE COURSE ALTERING NDE EXPERIENCES

A FORMER ATHEIST'S VIEW OF
HER DEATH EXPERIENCE

By Dr. Lotte Valentin N MD

The ER

It was the evening of July 12, 1992 and I was back in the ER due to hemorrhaging for three days after having given birth to my third child 12 days earlier. A doctor examined me and determined nothing much was happening at the moment as there was only a trickle of blood visible during the exam. They left me in the room, and I was to be held for observation. As I was lying in a pool of my own blood with the door shut and no bell to ring for help, a nurse finally came in to check on me. As she opened the door her jaw dropped as she realized how much I had been bleeding.

The panic that was written all over her face made me understand she knew something was terribly wrong. She quickly alerted the other doctors and nurses for help. I could hear the STAT call in the hospital loudspeakers as the call for OB GYN STAT TO THE

ER echoed on the speakers! Within a minute an out of breath middle-aged doctor ran into my room followed by a younger doctor. I remember feeling very relieved they had finally sent a doctor that looked like he had been through a few things in his profession and that he most likely would know what to do with me. This was the doctor that saved my life.

As they examined me another large blood clot surfaced, and I tried to sit up to tell him I wasn't feeling well. He quickly pushed me back down on to the bed, tipping me backwards in order to keep the blood in my head, heart, and vital organs. As this was taking place the room quickly filled with hospital staff and I could hear them all firing instructions of what to do next. There was a nurse on my left side trying to place an IV in my arm. On my right side there was a nurse who put a blood pressure cuff on my arm. I could feel myself fading away and getting weaker and weaker, and feeling like I was falling. I felt as if I had jumped out of an airplane without a parachute and was rapidly falling towards the ground.

I was mustering up every ounce I had within me to hold on to my life. Life, something I had been taking for granted was suddenly barely within reach. The nurse on my right was quoting my blood pressure and yelled out in a panicked voice, "50 OVER 15, HURRY"! My senses seemed superhuman and my hearing was so clear it was as if I was wearing some supernatural headphones. It was shortly after this moment that I realized I was dying. The KNOWING that I was dying was a very different feeling from THINKING I may die. As I was dying, I KNEW I was dying, there was no thinking "Oh my God, I'm going to die"! I was now in a complete state of sheer panic! There was a realization of I'M DYING! I felt myself getting weaker and weaker. I tried to hold on to my life with all my power. I felt like I was hanging off a cliff in the Grand Canyon using only my nails. Even though I was an atheist at the time I instinctively prayed to God to save my life. "I have three children under the age of six! They need a mother! Please let me live!" I pleaded with God! I felt like I was just rapidly falling in space. I struggled to hold on and stay inside my body.

The pull on my soul was too great and I found myself floating out of my body, hovering about two to three feet above myself. There was an instantaneous feeling of unconditional love and peace, and a knowing, that all of life was very divine. Everything made perfect sense on "the other side" as if I had knowledge of all that is, when outside my body. There was an understanding that I had access to all information past, present and future all at the same time. There was no time in the state I was in. I was in some kind of in-between state, not on Earth and not in heaven.

I felt as though there were a piece of me still in my body. I was somehow attached to my body even though I was hovering in space. There was a sense of an energetic attachment to the body as if my soul had just stepped outside its house temporarily, but you still knew you lived in the house. The first thing I noticed was that I was still alive. I was still there, just outside my body! How could this be I thought. How could I still be alive but without my body? How could I think and process what was happening without my body? All of a sudden, I was sucked back into my body, like a giant vacuum hose, similar to how Tim Allen in the movie Santa Claus goes through the chimney to deliver Christmas presents. I could feel the IV fluids rushing through my veins, like a cartoon figure undergoing surgery. Everybody in the room was clapping and cheering as I regained consciousness, like a Hospital TV show. I felt relieved I was back in my body. I had made it! I had survived!

First Encounter

I spent the next two days in the hospital. My head was pounding, and I was feeling very cold from not having enough blood in my body. As I was lying in the hospital room I was aware of my sister-in-law who had just passed three days earlier. I felt as though she was in the left corner of the ceiling looking down on me. There seemed to be some telepathic communication between us. She told me "You will be OK." I wondered if I was going crazy. I thought, how could I hear her? Was I really communicating with her? I wasn't sure what to believe, as I didn't have a scientific explanation for it. This is how my clairvoyance, clairaudience, and clairsentience began.

After this experience I became very sick and experienced bone marrow suppression. Every night when I went to bed, I would pray that I would wake up the next morning and there were days when I felt so weak and sick, I wished I would die. My daily experience was as if there were two separate parts to me: my body and my soul. I felt as though my soul was constantly trying to rise out of my body and I was walking a fine line between life and death.

The Light, The Music and The Spirit Guides

It had been a normal day of taking care of the children and dealing with my usual health struggles. As the evening approached we all went to bed performing the normal routine. In the middle of the night I woke up feeling weak and dizzy. I took my head off the pillow to lower it onto the mattress in order to increase the blood flow to my head. I was so tired of this existence and I just wanted to be healthy and normal again. I found myself struggling to keep my soul inside of me as usual but within a second my soul was pulled up and out!

For a brief moment I was floating outside my body but then quickly started to travel through darkness. It all happened so fast, just in a few seconds. I felt like I was flying through black empty space. My soul was travelling at lightning speed. I arrived at what I call a "mid-station" and somehow knew there were levels below me and above me. I was again still me, my soul, without my body. I was stunned to hear the most beautiful music. Music so beautiful it can't be made on the Earth plane.

I wondered where this beautiful music came from and I saw a little brown wooden log cabin on my right. I opened the door to look inside to see if the music came from the cabin, but the cabin to my surprise was empty. I looked to my left and saw another cabin, the exact same cabin I had seen to my right. I opened the door to look inside. To my surprise, this cabin was also empty. I wondered where the beautiful music came from and was made aware that the music and a very bright light were coming from behind me. My soul slowly turned around and I saw the most beautiful white light. The music was coming from the light. The light, so bright and magnificent I don't have words to describe it. There isn't any light on Earth that it can be compared to. There was unconditional love emanating from within it, and it felt as though I was part of it. The light was so peaceful, beautiful and radiant. It enveloped me. I was part of the light, and I wanted to stay there forever. It was so bright and so beautiful and just thinking of the music and white light brings tears to my eyes even today. It is what we come from, carry within us, and will return to. It is Sacred. It is Divine.

In the bright white light, I could see the outline of Angles. The music came from the Angels. As I didn't believe in angles, I was confused as to why I was seeing this. I was seeing things I didn't believe to be true. Why was this happening? All of a sudden there was a spirit guide on my right side that was communicating with another spirit guide on my left side using instantaneous telepathic communication. The spirit guide on my right said "What is she doing here? She can't be here! She has to go back!" As I could understand the communication I responded telepathically and said, "NO, WAIT!" How can this be? How can I be outside my body and still be me? How does this work?" The spirit guide on my left said, "If I told you, you wouldn't remember after going back, but you will remember this."

At this point an image appeared in front of me and I saw the Earth as if from outer space. There was a silvery glittery grid surrounding the Earth. At the time I thought it looked like a fish net surrounding the Earth as that is what it looked like to me having grown up laying fishing nets with my grandmother in the Atlantic Ocean. When my grandmother stood up in the rowing boat and lifted the nets out of the ocean the early morning sun would shine on the water droplets on the fishnet, making it glitter in the sunlight. The spirit guide on my left said, "Everything on Earth is connected to this grid and everything on Earth is connected to each other."

After this statement, I was sent back to my body at a rapid speed. I travelled at the same instantaneous speed as I had during my first NDE and was sucked back into my body with the same feeling of a strong vacuum hose. What had just happened? How could I just leave my body and have a spiritual experience and then just slip back into my body? How did all this work? As I laid there in bed trying to digest what had happened, my husband slept peacefully next to me, and I could hear my two-year-old waking up crying and I thought to myself, "OK so I had to be back in time for her waking up, my children need me, that's why they sent me back!"

Clairvoyancy – The Accident

After my NDEs I started seeing things before they happened. I had become clairvoyant. Right after I woke up one morning around the year 2001 I experienced a clairvoyant message. I was shown three images in successive order. The first image was of a large horizontal black scratch across the sliding door on the passenger side of our Van. I understood the image was showing me that we had been in an accident.

In the second image I was shown two of my children in the car, one in the front passenger seat and the other in the back seat. I knew the children were my two younger children who were at the time about twelve and nine years old. In the third image I saw myself leaving a note on the windshield of a black sedan car. I knew that none of us had been injured and I wasn't aware of any information regarding the passengers of the black sedan car. I thought it was very odd that I was leaving a note on the black car and wondered, "Where was the driver of the black car? Had the driver been injured and taken to a hospital? But if that driver was injured shouldn't there have been a police officer at the site?" I told my two younger children about my vision and we discussed the several possibilities where we could be involved in an accident.

We all felt it was most likely going to happen if we were making a left turn and had oncoming traffic that could collide with the right side of our car. There was only one likely intersection for such an accident that we could think of. As I drove them to San Francisco every day for their ballet lesson we would take the Bay Bridge across the water to San Francisco. As we would exit the bridge and head down on to the surface streets we would make a left turn, which had oncoming traffic. For about ten days we arrived at the traffic light of the suspected accident intersection and the children would anxiously look out their windows to make sure there were no oncoming traffic that could hit us.

After about 10 days of suspenseful driving we were in Walnut Creek at our local shopping center. We had done some shopping at the bookstore and when exiting the garage, there was a big truck parked on my left offloading boxes. I tried to squeeze by the big truck and out on to the narrow street making a right turn and there were several cars in line trying to enter the parking area. As I was turning right on to the street, the right side of my car, the passenger van door, scraped the black sedan car that was parked on the street. I immediately knew this was the accident I had seen and got out of my car to look at the damage. As I saw the black horizontal scratch across my van door I tilted my head backwards toward the blue sky and threw my arms up in the air and started to laugh out loud hysterically. The scratch on my door matched the image I had been shown two weeks earlier perfectly. Finally, I thought, no more worrying! The person offloading boxes on the truck as well as the pedestrians on the sidewalk and drivers in nearby cars just stared at me. They must have thought I was crazy as I was laughing at my own accident!

I left a note on the windshield of the black sedan car, to let the owner know my information. Nobody was hurt, it was just material damage, and we were all relieved the accident was over and we could stop worrying. Now I understood why I had not been shown the driver of the black sedan car! My life continued on like this and I became more and more clairvoyant, clairaudient, and clairsentient as time passed.

The Message

I had just turned forty-six and it was July 2004. My children were now 18, 15 and 12 and it was time to start thinking about what I wanted to do when returning back to the workforce. As I stood up from my computer in the living room and started to walk toward the kitchen I became aware of a spirit guide who was communicating with me. I stopped in the middle of the room and just stared up into the ceiling wondering if I would be able to see the spirit guide. I didn't see anything, but I could hear the spirit guide giving me messages telepathically and sensed a presence in the room. The spirit guide gave me four messages:

1. You have to become a Naturopathic Doctor.

2. You are to integrate East and West.

3. You will bring messages and healing to the people.

4. You will write two books, no wait, three.

The spirit guide continued.

You need to go to Medical School and become a Doctor first.

When the time is right we will tell you the next steps

You will know later on what the books and messages are about

The message was so strong and direct that I enrolled in Medical School Prerequisite classes within a week.

In 2012 at the age of 54 I had completed the pre-requisites and started medical school. In 2016 I received my license to practice Medicine. Now began my journey into mediumship, and after studying at the renowned Arthur Findlay College in England I became a working evidential psychic medium. Today I divide my time between working as a physician and working spiritually to help people find their own path to heal physically, emotionally, and spiritually, and to bridge the gap between science and soul.

We are all connected. We are all one. It is all Divine and so are you.

Dr. Lotte Valentin N.M.D., Phoenix Arizona

Dr. Lotte Valentin is an N.M.D., author, evidential medium, spiritual educator and an international keynote speaker! She teaches several different spiritual workshops as well as offering one-on-one sessions for mediumship, ancestral healing and as a medical intuitive.

She has experienced two out of body near-death Experiences, NDE's which led her to start medical school at age of 54. Dr. Lotte captivates her audiences and inspire them to become the person they were born to be by moving from their mind to their heart. Dr. Lotte also hosts her own podcast *Dr. Lotte: Science with Soul* to help people create a path to healing their own life physically, emotionally and spiritually, and bridge the gap between science and soul. She lives in

Phoenix, Arizona, where she operates Center for Integrative Medicine as well as her Spiritual Center, Divine Spiritual Essence.

www.drlotte.com

www.DivineSpiritualEssence.com

Facebook and Instagram @ Dr.LotteValentin

GOD IS LOVE

By Ritu Lebouef

A Spiritually Transformative Experience and the realization of the very essence of Sanatana Dharma or what is now popularly called Hinduism.

During one of those gatherings in the backroom one evening in March 1998, I went into a deep, long meditation. I didn't realize the session was over, and everyone had left the room. By the time I came out of meditation, I saw I was the only one in the room and it was 9pm, and time for the store to close. I hurriedly went toward the main entrance of the store to say good night to the bookstore owner, who was also in a hurry to wrap up and leave for the day.

That day I had hoped I'd talk to her and she might know the answer or guide me to a book in her store that would explain the symbolism of my dream. I felt slightly disappointed that I didn't have time to talk to the owner about the meaning of my dream, and despite the long deep meditation, I didn't get any insight into its meaning, or see, feel, or experience anything out of the ordinary, although overall, I was feeling very peaceful and pleasant.

Absentmindedly I went into the parking lot which was empty except for two cars. There was no other traffic on the road. It was calm weather, dark except for streetlights. I sat in my car, closed the door, put on my seatbelt, put the key in the ignition and turned it on.

That very instant there was a sound of a shockingly loud explosion. For a split second I thought my car had blown up or there was some bomb explosion.

First Phase

But amazingly I was still there and before I could react to the explosive sound anymore, I was soaking in Divine Love. It was as if the whole Universe had opened up 360°. It was all open Space, and it was the Whole Existence right there.

It is impossible to describe that Love. It was purer than pure. It was beyond my wildest imagination. It is not right to even call it love but there is no other word in the dictionary to describe it. This Love was not a part of the formless Existence. The Existence itself was Love. This Existence didn't have Love, it didn't express Love, IT was LOVE ITSELF. Nothing but pure Love.

It was as if this all-pervasive Love couldn't help but overflow. The Love from existence was overflowing nonstop, dripping love drops everywhere. Each Love Drop was taking a physical form. All of nature was forming out of the love drops. Each tree, each blade of grass, each dew drop, each insect, each human body, each drop of water was a physical manifestation of the invisible formless Love.

Everything, the whole Existence, was not just created and then filled with love (like jelly is filled in a Jelly donut), but the very substance of everything was made of Pure Love. The very essence, the very being of everything was Love.

During all this experience I had no awareness of my body. I don't know how much time had elapsed. I was not aware of any physical space either. I didn't have any thoughts at that time. I was in a total experiential state. It is only later I was able to think and give words to that experience.

Second Phase

When you change the gear in a standard shift car there is a slight pause and jerk. Almost kind of like that gear shift, there was a shift in my experience just as suddenly.

I became aware that I was in a vehicle even though I still had no awareness of anything physical including my body. This 'I' was more like an 'I' as an Awareness. My focus went to the space in front of me. It was as if I was in a vehicle flying at lightning speed in open dark space and billions of shimmering stars were flying toward my windshield from the opposite direction at lightning speed, too. They were not colliding with or touching the windshield. They were flying past my windshield.

Next, I became aware that I had been crying a lot, more like bawling. I still couldn't feel or sense my body, but I knew tears were flowing non-stop because I was overwhelmed with all the Divine Love. Again, I had no sense of actual physical space or time. The flying through space and stars went on for a long time.

Third Phase

Then another sudden shift occurred, again like a gear shift in a standard car. In a snap I was experiencing COMPLETE ONENESS with the Absolute. I was the Absolute.

I was no longer a separate awareness experiencing God, but I became IT. I was THAT. I was the Omnipresent LOVE! I was the FORMLESS ONE DRIPPING LOVE DROPS that were manifesting INTO FORM everywhere. All of it was me. I was in God and God was in me. We were One and the same. I was the formless and the form, all pervading and timeless. I was everything and nothing at the same time, beyond time and space, with no awareness of my body, any separate existence as a physical being, of the car I was in, or of surroundings.

Fourth Phase

Abruptly another major gear shift occurred. Similar to the Second Phase, I became aware of myself as a separate entity, although I still didn't sense my physical body, time, or space. I call this awareness MACRO ME and MINI ME.

I was the Absolute, everything, all Pervading and Eternal and simultaneously I was contained in a body self too. It was an extremely thrilling and exhilaratingly blissful feeling that "I," the all Pervading, was also the "I" in a physical body EXPRESSING ITSELF and EXPERIENCING ITSELF through the body and a specific personality.

I 'knew' I had a physical body and that body was behind the wheel of the car, but I couldn't exactly 'feel' my body. I knew I was driving but couldn't see or feel my arms or hands or my legs or any other physical body part.

Up until then, I was just having pure experience without any thinking or processing. But suddenly I had curiosity. I wondered, "If I can't feel any physical body I am in, then what is the part that is doing this thinking? Where is this awareness of experience coming from? Where is the part that is differentiating between the Cosmic/Macro Me and Mini Me?"

When I questioned that, I could sense some limited space over where my physical head would have been (had I been able to actually feel my physical body), where all these thoughts seem to be coming from.

Next, I became aware of Mini-Me being completely overwhelmed with the LOVE again. I was bawling with a non-stop stream of tears while questioning, "How do we humans forget this

Truth about ourselves? How do we get so separated from our True Selves? How can we commit horrendous crimes, hate, be violent, and inflict pain on others?" I was now also completely overwhelmed with pain about our collective non-loving ways. It was heart-wrenching.

Through all of this I was still whizzing through Space with billions of stars flying at lightning speed into the windshield without touching it and disappearing. I had no sense of time or physical space.

Through this heart-wrenching overwhelmed state, I continued to have no awareness of how much time had elapsed and how was I able to drive all the way from the bookstore to the house, on streets and highways. I never saw the 'road' in front of me, the little bit that I was aware of driving. It was only driving through billions of stars in Space flying by.

Fifth Phase

As soon as I pulled into my home driveway, put the car in park, and turned off the ignition, for the first time I became aware of physical space. I wasn't thinking about my body, but now I had a more concrete sense of it.

I locked the car and walked into the darkened house, and checked on my two sleeping toddlers, quietly walking into my son's room. He woke up a bit, and I quickly picked him up before he started crying, rocking him gently while sitting on the edge of the bed. He fell asleep again, and I laid him back on his bed.

I was still soaking in love. I do not remember changing my clothes and getting into the guest bed so no one would be disturbed, and shortly after laying down, I sat back up. By this time, it was probably between 10pm-10:15pm.

Sixth Phase

As soon as I sat up, the temporarily-halted experience restarted. It was as if the whole experience was on a temporary pause and now the play button was pushed again but differently.

I was Love. Every fiber of my being was bursting with Love. Love was pouring into me. I started hearing ancient Sanskrit chants. I felt the presence of sages chanting all around my head and in the space above my head, like they were doing Yagnas (Holy Fire Sacred ceremonies). It wasn't physical sound, but awareness of their presence and sounds.

Simultaneously there were unearthly smells, like sandalwood incense. They were extremely strong in my nostrils and going up my forehead, my eyes were probably closed, and I didn't have any sense of my physical body. Every nerve, every cell, every fiber of my being was vibrating with these overpowering sounds, presences, smells and Love. I felt I couldn't contain it anymore. I felt I would blow up or burst into a billion pieces. My senses couldn't handle the power of this experience.

I tried and tried and tried but I reached a point where I felt I couldn't take the experience anymore without exploding into billions of pieces. At that moment I silently cried within myself, "I can't take this anymore." That very instant everything stopped and disappeared, the sounds, the smells, the bursting with Love.

I was still soaking in this love, but simultaneously exhausted. Perhaps all the crying had me exhausted. I didn't check the time, but it must have been around 3am or 4am because I had a short and very refreshing sleep until it was daytime, and I needed to wake up.

Questions

I also wonder if I actually went into deep meditation for a while when I sat up in bed and then the experience of sounds and smells began. Looking at the duration I was sitting up and how incredibly overpowering the experience was, I wonder how I could have gone through it for so many hours.

I obviously drove the car for 40 minutes from the bookstore to my house on highways and streets, but I have no conscious knowledge of how the car got driven.

At the time of that experience I was already a disciple of an Enlightened Master and a perfect Yogi, my Guru Swami Mohan Das Ji Maharaj, who lived in India. I rarely ever had any conversations with him. Back in 1982 when I had asked him spiritual questions, he had told me, "All answers are within you. Go and experience them for yourself." Therefore, he gave me no verbal or written guidance or explanations, but afterwards in the year 2000 he told me that I had a true and valid experience.

Life Changes

Although I was in a successful upwardly-mobile IT career which I loved, I couldn't continue with it anymore. Following a career or pursuit of wealth lost all meaning. I knew I needed to focus on spiritual growth and be an energy healer. Even though it was a huge challenging shift to give up a big paycheck and there was a lack of support for my decision, I didn't continue with my IT career.

- During my healing practice I noticed flashes of intuitive ability, of clairaudience, clairsentience, and knowledge of tissue massage and reflexology. I had enthusiasm to formally learn these modalities which I would have never considered earlier. Miraculous healings happened through me. I was able to help many people.

- I was able to give inspired guidance to people when they asked. I knew I wasn't speaking from my mind, but words of guidance were coming through me. I realized the impact of compassionate listening in the overall healing of a person.

- Gradually I realized that it was more important for me to offer spiritual mentoring because living from spiritual perspective and awareness could automatically heal people at all levels. Although I am an introvert and a loner and I was a very quiet and timid, I felt driven to make internal and external shifts, howsoever slowly, to be able to share my spiritual message globally.

- Prior to the experience, I used to have frequent medical health issues. I have been able to use the wisdom and knowledge of this experience as an anchor to navigate very difficult situations and heal mentally, emotionally, and physically.

Most importantly I realized the very essence of Sanatana Dharma. (Sanatana Dharma is the original name of what is now popularly called Hinduism). By its very nature Sanatana Dharma is a Sanskrit term that is devoid of sectarian leanings or ideological divisions. Sanatana means Eternal and Dharma is not translatable to any other language. Its approximate meaning is "Natural Law," or those principles of reality which are inherent in the very nature and design of the universe. Therefore, Dharma can be roughly translated as The Way, The Universal Truth, The Divine Order. Hence Sanatana Dharma is The Eternal Universal Truth. Within it is the most famous expression of the relationship between the individual and the Absolute. 'Aham Brahmasmi (I am Brahman/That' Tat tvam asi, "thou art that")

Ritu LeBouef India, Dallas, Texas, USA

Spiritual Mentor, Certified Life Coach, Reiki Master, Registered Massage Therapist, Blogger, Speaker and author of an upcoming book (title TBD) which will answer the question Who Am I and give clarity into the Nature of Mind and provide ways to balance it for healing and greater self-awareness.

Ritu@spiritualroute.co
www.spiritualroute.com
www.youtube.com/spiritualroute
www.facebook.com/spiritualroute

LONGING FOR THE LIGHT

How I Found the Books I Was Promised in my Near-Death Experience!

By Lilia Samoilo

Since 2012, I have been educating the international community about combat soldiers' and others near-death experiences (NDEs) and spiritually transformative experiences (STEs) with Dr. Diane Corcoran of IANDS (International Association for Near-Death Studies)

While reading the IANDS monthly email February 2017 STE account, I experienced an intense life-changing spontaneous event that produced a latent, indelible recall of my childhood NDE and life's mission. Confused and needing answers about this experience, I reached out to Diane. She said that I had an STE that led to a spontaneous recall of my first NDE from age 3.

She asked me to write an article for the IANDS community describing the STE, my NDE, and the recall of my life's mission of telling the world about the set of books I was told I would find one day that would lead to the Ascension. I told her that I had found the books promised and have been studying them for nearly forty years because of their profound impact on my life. I explained that these books are filled with instruction that explain the Cosmic Laws of the Universe, and as a mental health and spiritual counselor, I felt they would help to validate and answer many questions experiencers have following their NDEs and STEs. I mentioned that Dr. Wayne Dyer was so impacted by one of these same books, (Volume 3 of the Saint Germain Series, The "I AM" Discourses), that he published many of its quotes in his book, *Wishes Fulfilled*. He often read sections from this same volume to audiences all over the world, until his passing.

My story begins with describing the STE that led to a spontaneous recall of my NDE at age three and the re-awakening of my life's purpose. After I read the February 2017 STE account, it provoked powerful wave after wave of pulsating, magnetic-like sensations that coursed through every cell of my mind and body. Basking within a glorious, magnificent radiance beyond splendor, beyond words, it took everything within me to remain still, as I quietly accepted what I can only refer to as a perfect state of ecstasy, a co-union or communion with Living Light and Love. The energy was magnificent, vibrant, radiant, active, and supremely "present." The Source of this radiating Essence was very familiar to me. It was the Great Presence of Light and Power enveloping me in an avalanche of Its Perfect Love. Simultaneously, with this recognition, a spontaneous awakening had occurred, as if all at once, a living "signal" ignited in my heart. It was the very signal I had unknowingly, long awaited since my childhood NDE.

I began recalling some of the details of that NDE, including the re-awakening of my life's purpose, and the "knowing" that I would search for, and one day find the books that taught the Great Laws of Life, Light, Love and Perfection and would point me to the way of permanent freedom — the Ascension.

The signal I experienced was "THE" cue for me to begin telling others about this same set of books called the Saint Germain Series. But, being such a private person, the thought of sharing any part of my experience, let alone my personal spiritual beliefs in public, filled me with such self-doubt and trepidation, that my heart began pounding in my chest. As I obeyed the urge to sit quietly, a great sense of loving peace poured over me. All my reservations and objections of sharing this event and telling others about the books subsided. Within minutes following this event, whenever attempting to process my experience, I re-lived, in part, the same blissful ecstasy that I felt during my experience.

My first experience regarding these books began with my first NDE at the age three.

My siblings, my grandmother and I often walked to a nearby cemetery to feed the squirrels that pranced about a beautiful white Greek-style pavilion courtyard surrounded by a colorful, panoramic, plush garden of flowers and shrubbery. One day, I decided to bring a shoe box to catch a squirrel for a pet. I recall chasing them, as they weaved about the tombstones to dodge me. As my brother abruptly pulled the box from my hands, I began falling toward a tombstone. At once, I was somehow above my body "matter-of-factly" watching the scene play out in slow motion. Just before my head struck the tombstone, I was removed from the scene. I was knocked unconscious for hours.

The next memory I had was being above a child's body that was lying motionless on a couch in a large room, with a white cloth draped across its forehead. Near the child was a woman, fretfully praying to God for the child to awaken. I felt neither emotion nor attachment to the child, its surroundings, or the praying woman. While I was there observing, I was not a child, nor a body. I was just pure consciousness and energy, without ego or a sense of time or space. I existed in the "Now" surrounded by a very familiar, blissful atmosphere of peace and contentment. I was part of a Conscious Intelligence, an Essence, an Awareness, a Presence of Light, placed there above the child, to observe the praying woman for the child's sake. I saw light emanating from the lady's body as she prayed. Her imploring words to God to bring the child back were the only thing I focused my attention upon, and then in an instant, I was back in the child's body. I felt repulsed being "stuffed" back into that baby body. As I open my eyes, I was moaning in great pain from a massive headache. Only then did I recognize the woman as my aunt and that I was lying on the couch in my living room. My aunt raced to my side, hugging and kissing me, weeping thankfully to God, out loud, that I had finally opened my eyes.

Though I do not recall much of the details of what took place while I lay unconscious, I do recall in my feelings, that where I was taken and taught in the Light was very familiar to me, and that it was not of this world. I walked away from that experience longing for the Light more than ever, almost aching to return to it, knowing that the Light was my true home and that I was always connected to it. After that experience, I began living from the "heart-level" of life, knowing that the answers I sought would be found in the Light. Thereafter, I had numerous experiences encouraging me, while I continued searching for the set of books that would lead to the Ascension. The anticipation of becoming free, going "home" eternally, to this day remains paramount to my life! As Jesus stated in the Gospel of John, "...know the truth and the truth shall make you free."

Since a very young age, I recall having had many impactful, oftentimes dangerous close calls with death and numerous vivid STEs that eventually led me to find the books. Preceding every close call with death, I would be given a premonition of danger, at times given an audible command or direction that spared my life. During each event, I was aware of the same Great Presence of Love and Light that would swoop in to grab, push, or cradle me out of danger's way like it did in my childhood NDE. Rapid changes or shifts in consciousness and feeling followed each close call and STE, as if a string of dormant "Deja-vu" memories were being played out, reminding me of my life's mission regarding the instruction taught in the books.

These shifts in consciousness included developing new specific sets of skills and insights that I have used as a counselor and minister, to assist others with their life's journey and purpose. Each of my experiences served as proof that we are all loved unconditionally, and are part of, and permanently connected to the same Great One Source of God's Life, and returning to it permanently, by the way of the Ascension is our destiny.

Voila! After many years of searching for the books, at age 19, I was handed Volume 1 of the *Saint Germain Series*, Unveiled Mysteries. I took it home that evening and was so positively thrilled to be "reunited" with the instruction, that I read the entire book that night! Upon returning the book, my friend looked at me with disappointment, assuming that I had not read it, since he only loaned it to me the previous night. I reassured him that I read the entire book and had only one question for him. I asked, "If I follow this instruction described in this book, can I make my Ascension? When he responded "yes," my search was over.

Studying these books for the past forty years has had an indelible impact on my life because they provided the understanding I long sought about the purpose of Life. All of my being is perfectly aligned with it, and I thank God every day for keeping His promise to me about finding the pathway to the Ascension. How does one describe the thrill of finally finding what was promised? Being reunited with the books and the Great Ones who brought them forth was beyond thrilling. There are no adequate words to describe the thrill. Just ask any experiencer who has been embraced by the Light. Finding, studying, and applying the Cosmic Laws taught in the books on a daily basis has been the most powerful, profound, and impactful experience of my life. I feel privileged to finally share them with those searching for answers to questions about life and their experiences in the Light.

What I was told to share with others

The Light is REAL and Eternal! There is no such thing as so-called death because our connection to the Source of All Light and Love is Eternal. The Ascension is achievable! And the "I AM" Instruction, as described in the Saint Germain Series Books, is the true education of Life, as it is the Whole of the Law. It educates humanity about the Laws of Light, Love and Perfection that govern all Life. In an easy-to-understand manner, it explains how to attain the Ascension, and describes our direct connection with our own individual Source from whence we all have come, the Great Source of our life, the Great "I AM." This Presence of Light is often referred to as the Guardian Angel, of which many experiencers have reported seeing or being amidst, during their NDE or STE.

Are NDEs & STEs imaginary or real?

In my own opinion, as a life-long multiple NDEr and STEr, counselor, minister, NDE educator and author, returning to the Light in these events is not imaginary but real, and is as natural as a child turning to its mother. They are "organic" events that serve a great purpose to those who experience them and all who wish to learn more about them. They serve to reconnect experiencers with their True Source of All Life and the Great Laws that govern them. While in the Light, they are often given a life review, the reason why they are sent back to their bodies, and whatever they need to help them advance to the next step of fulfilling their Divine Plan.

Since NDEs and STEs are real to the experiencer, they should be validated as such. To not do so is to "deconstruct the purpose" of which their event serves. Doesn't it make sense that since we are part of the Light, that whenever a trauma or a life event triggers an NDE or STE, we naturally "return" to our Source of Light often referred to as "home" by experiencers? Why is it that once being embraced by the Lights' indescribable, unconditional love and comfort, experiencers resist returning to their bodies when told, "It is not yet your time?" Why do they no longer fear death? Why do they "long" to return home again? Why do they experience a life review? Why does their experience become indelible, remaining as vivid as the moment they experienced it? Why do they come back immensely changed and often with new talents or abilities?

Experiencers looking for validation and answers to their questions regarding their events, and those seeking answers to their questions about the meaning of life may find their answers just as I did, in these books. The instruction contained within them is the "Whole of the Law," teaching humanity where God abides, what the Power of God is, how to use that Power, and what humanity is supposed to do with it. Practicing the way to attain it, as described in the Saint Germain Series, is as simple as studying and applying the laws of mathematics, which solve every problem with perfect results.

As far as I am concerned, working with Diane and IANDS was destiny.

Their 2017 STE account provoked the re-awakening of my life's purpose. Only now do I realize that my initial contact with Diane years ago was "meant -to- be," -a very necessary, crucial step needed to help fulfill my mission of telling the world, especially active military, veterans, and others who have had NDEs and STEs about these wonderful educational books of Light!

It means the world to me that God kept His promise of my finding the Saint Germain Series books. I plan to keep my promise to Him and tell the world about them and their impact on my life.

Lilia Samoilo

Lilia Samoilo is a child NDEr, a multiple adult NDEr and has had a lifetime of STEs, shared NDEs, as well as being a medical and spiritual intuitive. She is a Minister and a Mental Health and Spiritual Counselor for nearly forty years devoting her life to educating others about our Eternal connection to our Source, the Power of One, and the Infinite Power of Love. In addition to Lilia's major contribution to the International Association For Near-Death Studies and the Vet NDE Project, she is best known for her work as an international Vet NDE Advocate, NDE Educator and being the Associate Producer of NDE Radio with Lee Witting.

Since 2013, she began raising global awareness of NDEs and the medical and spiritual gap of care of NDErs to medical professionals, clergy and the general public. Lilia was a major contributor and commentary author for the Narrative Inquiry in Bioethics' NDE Symposium and her article was published in MUSE, by Johns Hopkins University *Press,* Volume 10, Number 1, Spring 2020, pp. 37-42 on a term and topic she coined, *Closing the Medical & Spiritual Gap of Care for Patients Who Have Had a Near-Death Experience.* Her commentary article educates healthcare professionals, researchers, clergy and the general public about NDEs, their aftereffects, and how to specifically prevent and close the medical and spiritual gap of care for NDErs. For years, Lilia has volunteered her counseling, consulting, booking agent skills, media and marketing expertise to help support and promote IANDS, NDE related communities, NDErs, STErs and NDE-related authors, filmmakers, Guidepost's NDE Book Series, podcasts and radio hosts. Email Lilia at longing4thelight@outlook.com.

To order the authentic green-colored books of the Saint Germain Series, *Unveiled Mysteries, The Magic Presence, The "I AM" Discourses,* by Godfre Ray King, contact the Saint Germain Press: order@SaintGermainPress.com or call 847-882-1911 US CST. Also available on Amazon.

I must add a side bar here about Lilia,

I have never met anyone with the fortitude and strength of character as this amazing person.

Our meeting, and the fruition of this book was guided by the Stars. Call it Happenstance, Circumstance or Synchronicity, I agree with Albert Einstein that 'Coincidence is God's way of Remaining Anonymous', as Lilia would prefer to be. Still, I must thank her from the bottom of my heart for all she has done for me and the collection of stories for this book.

THE DAY I STOOD AT HEAVEN'S DOOR

(After ignoring my intuition)

By Alan R Stevenson

" **A** fter coming back, I fell in Love with all that there is, from all that I had learned." Alan R. Stevenson

I wish I could say the day I died was just another ordinary day so it would appear more literarily dramatic. Instead, like an ironic preview of coming attractions, the day was besieged by the only snowstorm of the winter season in the Niagara Peninsula. For me, it was a prelude to the inevitable reality that each of us will someday face. It is a day that some consider while others fear it to an extreme.

February 26, 2010 is only a short distance behind me now that I've spent some time in the sun amongst the care of loved ones. I am grateful for having had a peaceful space to do my healing of body, mending of mind, sorting of soul, and learning of lessons about what "being" means.

That morning was quite different, in that the fabric of my physical world appeared somewhat out of sync. Under ordinary circumstances, most would be oblivious to these minute details. Pain from what I assumed was severe heartburn had lingered for three days. It was driven by a less than ideal life situation, ignoring the pain although I knew deep down I shouldn't. It was here. I first stepped into the conflicting pothole, having prioritized work over my health. I got ready for work, my routine unchanged except for the sluggishness that dogged me as I put on my winter boots.

Seized with a powerful sense of apprehension at venturing out into the bitter-cold Canadian weather, I still ignored the instincts that relentlessly nagged me. Thanks to a financial crisis where ends already did not meet and a work schedule that had me off for the previous six days, I was compelled to ignore my inner voice and layer up to deal with the harsh weather. What my internal voice couldn't convince me of, the increasing pain of even the simplest movement began to.

The thought of walking six blocks in the snowstorm only worsened my physical discomfort. For a fleeting moment, I thought of asking my younger brother for help, as he was in the living room watching the morning news.

Unfortunately, I had already envisioned his typical, "Suck it up buttercup," response to anyone mentioning a personal problem or hardship of any nature. Quickly dismissing the thought, I pulled my coat over my bulky layers and with a sense of great sadness, slipped my hat and gloves on.

Even as I opened the door to a blizzard and freezing temperatures, the sense of my impending doom hovered on the fringe of my awareness. The inexplicable sadness began to overwhelm me, and the raw emotion was yet another warning. Ignoring it with stoicism, I simply stepped outside and closed the door to the first opportunity to save my life. I didn't say anything to my brother, not even a simple goodbye, as tension was still high following an argument two days earlier, the cause as trivial as most were.

The blasting wind and snow intensified. Clutching the collar of my coat to my cheek, I cleared the steps of the front porch. I churned my feet through the foot-deep snow, making my way over to the main street. With my head bowed, the biting winds still teared up my eyes. Even in optimal health, walking across town as I usually did wasn't an option on such a brutal day. The agony in my chest had reached a disorienting level so I stopped at the store around the corner to grab a roll of antacid tablets, though it was against my better judgment. I simply knew I needed some kind of relief at that point — hell, anything!

While waiting behind another customer paying for their purchases, the store clerk, whom I knew fairly well, glanced at me several times with concern. Once again, an opportunity to save my life was presenting itself, if I would have simply asked for help. There was no excuse. I'd had many conversations with the clerk over the past six months and knew that he had been a paramedic back in his native Serbia. He had been unable to qualify as a paramedic in Canada due to his English. The sad and ironic thing about that, was his English was better than most born here.

His eyes never left me as I struggled to open the antacid roll. I barely remember paying for them, and as he counted the change, his eyes carefully assessed me. "Are you all right?" "Oh, I'm okay." "You don't look too well," he said more firmly.

Though his words registered in my pain-wracked mind, denial fought me on every front of my deteriorating condition, challenging all my common sense.

"I'll be all right," I insisted, though in truth a feeling of sheer dismay coupled with an emotional hopelessness had my thoughts flitting and flirting. All the while, the emotional roller coaster sped up to the point where it felt as though it would come off the tracks at any moment. Concentrating on the antacid package, it was all I could do to keep it together. Finally succeeding, I headed for the door while popping several tablets into my mouth. The regularly simple task of pushing open the door was as overwhelming as pushing a car, and once again I sidestepped an opportunity to save my life.

I stepped into the ferocious storm to walk six blocks through weather conditions I had not seen in years. My feet dragged like lead weights; it was all but impossible to lift them from the steadily deepening snow. With each step, the vise of dismay tightened its grip on my chest even further. My mind searched for solutions within the pain-induced fog, as my ego barged to the surface of my thoughts and screamed, "This isn't the day and nothing's going to happen to me!"

Struggling down Lake Street just past the armories, I looked around to determine how far I was from the bus stop and realized in heart-sinking fashion that I was completely alone in the storm. There wasn't a single soul to be seen anywhere, no cars, no people, no businesses open. Only the bone-chilling wind, driving snow, and excruciating pain. I felt more alone than I had ever felt or truly been before. To this day, I still clearly remember my instincts shouting, "You need to get to the hospital!" I persisted in the foolish belief that if I could just keep on keeping on, the episode would pass, and I might be okay after all.

Making it to the bus stop felt like a victory, though now I had to wait for the delayed bus. When it arrived and I boarded, I slipped the coins into the slot, and realized as it lurched away into the snow that everything had changed from one heartbeat to the next. I sagged into a seat a couple rows back behind the driver, becoming severally diaphoretic (sweating profusely) at this point. My ability to physically move was reduced to slow motion, as my hands wouldn't obey my struggles to remove my gloves, coat, and hat. With a grim understanding, I knew I had no choice but to ask for help now or die, and even with the cold truth staring me in the face, I couldn't immediately bring myself to act. Once again my instincts screamed at me to ask for help. Who knew how the mind and body truly acted under duress until faced with the most-dire circumstances?

Without thought, as the bus driver's eyes met mine in the mirror that hung above her, I asked her to call 911. She asked only why as she picked up the on-board phone. In a faltering voice I told her I was having a heart attack. Turning slowly, I noticed a woman sitting across from me. A horrified expression filled her round face as she clutched her bulky purse tightly to her chest.

The pain began dissipating rapidly as a serene peacefulness gently enveloped me. My gaze slowly lowered to my boots, and I thought, "So this is what it's like to die." During that transitory thought, I died. My vision winked into darkness as all the pain I had suffered over the past three days vanished without worry, anxiety or fear. The calm peacefulness strengthened, replacing all the pain of the moments before.

Then slowly, a misty opening began to appear about six inches or so in diameter in front of me. My mind was clear, and I felt light as air, as a strong sense of fascination engulfed my being and I felt a slow, easy, sideways movement with only the slightest pressure around me. Glancing down, I noticed that I had four arms and hands, four legs and feet. One set was more densely proportioned while the others were translucent appendages hovering just outside my physical body.

At this point, my long-time guardian, a tiger nearly six feet tall at the shoulder, stepped out of the near-blizzard conditions onto the bus. It seemed odd, but I knew him from other encounters during my life. Tiger is a soul guardian or what is known as 'a protector of souls.' He approached me and lovingly rubbed his head on the left side of my face. Slowly drawing back, he looked into my eyes and spoke in my mind.

"You are about to die."

He turned his head toward the windows, where holographic images displayed events from the past, present, and future, slowing to images of my two daughters. He looked back at me and said, "If you choose to."

"So I have a choice?" I asked in confusion. "Yes, you do. All of you have a choice. Everyone is given a choice with no judgment passed either way. Where you have been, where you are, and where you are going at all times is of your own choice."

I was overwhelmed by an emotional summary of my life, which we must all experience, whether staying or coming back. The best way to describe it would be to take every thought and feeling you've ever had, and every physical action you've ever done, then place it all into one emotional category. Ask yourself which emotion best sums up your life to date. Mine was marked by guilt for wasting my many talents and, in turn, my life.

We gazed deeply into each other's eyes and in a soft, submissive tone I replied, "I want to stay. I want to live." "Very well," Tiger said. "Now you have a task."

Tiger turned to leave as the thought flowed freely to me to follow. I didn't actually get up or walk anywhere, but we instantly traveled far to a place shrouded in a luminous, white mist. As we arrived, Tiger stepped ahead of me, turning to face me at an angle. Out on the fringe of my left peripheral vision, three Beings appeared, whom I've come to refer to as the Beings of 111 or 3. Once I focused my attention on them, they vanished. But when I looked at Tiger they reappeared, only to vanish once again as I turned toward them. It reminded me of gazing at a distant star in the night sky. If you look directly at it, it seems to wink out of sight, but reappears if you look a bit off and away from it.

Here began my first lesson with Tiger. I was emotionally searching for understanding as to why I could, yet couldn't, see the three Beings. "It does not matter," Tiger whispered. He then informed me the central Being was a Teacher, not only to myself, but to the other two Beings present. Eventually, they will become teachers themselves. The Teacher is an original consciousness (or child if you prefer) of what most refer to as God.

There are some important details readers must understand at this point. First, time as we perceive it does not exist. It is but a way to measure distance, such as the distance light travels in a year, or the sun traversing the sky from horizon to horizon. For point of reference sake, however, we shall stick with time as it is traditionally understood. I died at roughly 9:25am and was about to spend what would be considered a day's worth of time on the other side, prior to coming back to physical reality roughly ten minutes later, at 9:35am.

I was soon to understand the purpose of coming to this place as my focus intensified to such an extreme level that I felt anything and everything was possible. Tiger acted as the conduit for most of what was to follow. A little to my right, several holographic, free flowing images with full background appeared. Several times during the projection of images I would lack a clear understanding of the point being made. I would say in my mind "Yes, but…"at which point Tiger would patiently exclaim, "It does not matter." Finally, I began to understand that phrase was an important teaching and learning tool. There are things that truly are important, and then there are those that simply are not. The point at which you learn to make that distinction will free you to become the Being you were always meant to be.

Tiger escorted me back to the bus, as it was time for me to return. I thanked him for sharing insights and truths with me. He once again rubbed his head against mine with intense love before turning and leaving the bus. I haven't seen nor sensed him in any way since that moment he slinked his way off the bus.

As my physical reality started to return I saw the bus driver standing before me distraught and exclaiming, "What can I do? I think he's dead!"

With my physical reality returning to me, I became fully aware of the pain and surrounding environment. The first paramedic stepped onto the bus and asked a few questions to assess my condition. I felt incredibly relieved that someone had finally come to help me. When he turned and left the bus, I was filled with such dread that I screamed in my mind, "Please don't leave me now," but he was only returning to the ambulance to retrieve more equipment. The bus driver waited beside me until the paramedics returned. A frenzy of activity ensued while three of them worked to stabilize me enough to transport me to the hospital.

At St. Catharine's General Hospital, a doctor and nurse proceeded to inject, spray, and administer a vast amount of medication once the severity of my biological condition had been diagnosed. Then came the frantic orders from the trauma doctor, "Go! Go! Go! Get him out of here now!" Off I went to the more distant Hamilton General for heart surgery to save my life. It was a straight run down the Queen's Highway, the journey hastened by the urgent sirens on what would have otherwise been at least a thirty-minute drive. Through the windows of the rear door, I watched cars vanish as though they were standing still, and I realized how fast we were traveling.

The nurse sitting beside me looked at both paramedics flanking me and said, "We don't want to alarm you as you need to stay as calm as you can," then glancing at the cellphone on my lap, she added, "but if you wish to call someone, now would be the time to do that." My eyes welled up as I admitted that my cellphone had been disconnected the day before. She quickly retrieved hers and asked for a number to dial for me. I mentally searched for the first choice to call, but at the same time I didn't want to upset anyone. That was one of the hardest decisions I had to make, but I knew my daughters needed to know how much I loved them and what they had meant to me during the time they had shared my life.

Giving the nurse their mother's number at work, she tapped each number on the keyboard as I struggled to remember, then she passed the phone to me. Once Deb answered, I immediately apologized and explained the situation, then I relayed the message she needed to hear from me. I also told her that although things had not worked out as we had planned many years before, I cared deeply for her and would continue to do so no matter what ultimately happened to me, and I let her go with a deep sense of love. I envisioned the stoic expression on her face that would have concealed her distress, but I really had no idea what transpired in those few moments after I hung up.

When we arrived at the hospital, the paramedics rushed me through the blowing snow into the ER and down the hallways to an operating room. As I lay on the operating table, the OR staff stripped me down completely and prepped me for surgery, and a very young-looking surgeon approached and slightly leaning over me asked, "What the hell are you doing on my table?"

With my last ounce of quick wit, I said, "I'm having a bad day." He smiled a little and walked away for a short time. When he returned, he said, "Your left artery is one-hundred percent blocked. Medically, you had no reason to have survived what's known as a 'widow-maker' heart attack." I looked at him intently (with an unintentionally dreary gaze, considering all the chemicals that had been pumped into my body) and calmly said, "Oh, but I do."

I slowly regained consciousness late that evening. I emerged from a somewhat foggy state to a sense of peace. A minor physical discomfort was still present, though only in the background of my awareness. Awaking in a large ICU room, it was there I began to realize and feel the magical sense of being alive and all the magic a day holds. Over the following week in the hospital, gifts that I had returned with became apparent. "Gifts" may be the wrong term, as they are merely innate abilities in all, but for me they were life-changing legacies of my experience.

Alan Stevenson, Ontario Canada

Shortly after his 2010 near-death experience Alan put a draft of his eye-opening experience on the internet. Within a few months people around the world began finding him seeking help and advice. He enjoys sharing his experiences speaking at different sized gathering over the past decade, and is a true writer at heart and continues to work on other book projects. Contact Alan at: alanrstevenson.com

*Alan's use of the word 'Gifts' really rings true for me as I have acknowledged what I brought back with me from the beyond was 'Gifts' as well.

A spiritually-transformative experience (STE) is so powerful it may change your sense of who you are and what your true purpose on earth is about. It may also motivate you to transform your relationships as well as your work—and engage in new ways of living.

The following true-story is included as a chapter in my book: "A Brightly Guided Life: How A Scientist Learned to Hear Her Inner-Wisdom." To add context to this story, some new information has been added that was not included in the published version.

Ingrid Honkala, PhD

Chapter Five

SPIRITUALY TRANSFORMATIVE
EXPERIENCES OF PROTECTION

THE BEINGS OF LIGHT AND THE DISAPPEARANCE OF THE BODY

By Ingrid Honkala, PhD

After having a near-death experience when I was almost three years old, I started to have visions and out of body experiences, and to communicate with what I called "Beings of Light," all of which have continued for the rest of my life.

At the age of eighteen, when I was in college, I was meditating in my bed when I had a panoramic vision of a bedroom where a man was resting on the bed. I didn't know where the room was, or the man's identity.

The Beings of Light responded, "You are going to meet."

"Why? Who is this guy? Where and when are we meeting?" I inquired.

"Soon, on campus. You are going to help each other a great deal."

As I came closer to him I was able to see his face clearly. His green eyes were bright and beautiful.

"Wow, he is a beautiful being. Okay, I want to meet him," I said, feeling joyful.

A couple of weeks later I met him at the cafeteria, where he was eating lunch with some of his buddies. When I saw him, I recognized him immediately and I sat at the table right in front of him. I looked at him and as he returned a gaze into my eyes, I smiled. At first he barely smiled back, but after we looked at each other again we both smiled, then I stood up and waved goodbye.

We didn't talk that day, but later that week we met again at the cafeteria and then we introduced ourselves. His name was Santiago, and he was studying Industrial Design.

His eyes were as profound and beautiful as in my vision, making me feel very comfortable in his presence. He liked me too, so we quickly became close friends. We dated for a couple of weeks until I told him that I really wasn't into the boyfriend-girlfriend kind of relationship; then we broke up. At the beginning, he didn't take the news well. But we had already learned so much about each other and felt so good together that we remained friends. For the very first time in Santiago's life, he had been able to talk openly with someone about his deepest feelings of sadness and anger, and I was so happy knowing that I was there not just to listen, but to offer guidance.

Santiago was born with a genetic defect that made his blood vessels grow abnormally on almost half of his body including his face. So part of the left side of his face was covered with a dark purple blotch that he called "The Stain." Due to his condition he was very insecure about his appearance and was holding a lot of anger within himself. He couldn't understand why he had come into this harsh world to carry this kind of suffering. According to him, life was unfair.

When I met Santiago, he was a very analytical and skeptical person, which was something I was used to encountering. So when I mentioned to him anything about metaphysics, he tried at first to deny that anything in that realm was possible. This behavior soon stopped when I told him that I was able to travel with my mind and see other places.

"Do you mean astral traveling? I have heard of that, but I don't believe it is possible," he exclaimed.

Then I proceeded to describe his bedroom in great detail to him, even though I had never been there in person. After his jaw dropped in disbelief, I told him something that I had once learned from the Beings of Light:

"Doubt everything, but always keep an open mind. An open mind has the potential to make great discoveries."

"Okay, I'll give it a try," he replied.

I told him about my spiritual groups and I invited him to come with me to TM (Transcendental Meditation) and MAIS (Alternative Movement for Indian Social Studies). About two months into our friendship, he joined the groups and began to meditate for the very first time. Not long after, we started to experience amazing things together.

On one occasion when we were deeply immersed in a conversation about the chakras, I felt a tingling sensation in my hands. When I opened them right in front of Santiago, tiny sparks of light were coming from my palms,. shining very brightly like glitter, before vanishing into the air. We looked at each other in amazement. After grabbing my hands he said, "I want some of that light."

"You already have it," I stated. "We are all surrounded by it. I told you already that I could see auras." "I know for a fact that everything is made of matter and energy, but how is it possible that energy can manifest like that?"

"I am telling you, everything is possible. Just keep an open mind."

The same thing happened to us a few more times. Santiago would always try to find the most logical explanation, which sometimes led us into conflict.

"Ingrid, I am trying to have an open mind about all of this, but I think that these phenomena must have some kind of scientific explanation," he said.

"Stop putting rationality into everything," I would protest. "Not everything can be explained like that..."

"Yes, there is much about humanity that we still don't know," he interrupted, "but I am sure that everything has a logical explanation."

Still in disagreement, we decided not to discuss this issue anymore. I thought if he only knew half of the things I know he would realize how limited the rational mind can be.

About a week later we met to go to the MAIS meeting together. To catch the bus we had to walk a few blocks. We were distracted chatting when we saw three homeless people across the street, carrying big blankets around their bodies and looking disheveled.

When they noticed us, they crossed the street and came toward us. In Colombia, homeless people were responsible for much of the brutal street crime. Feeling frightened, Santiago and I held each other's hands.

"Let's keep going, maybe they will let us go," Santiago whispered.

As they got closer I saw that they were all men. The closer they came, the more I invoked the presence of the Beings of Light.

When the three men surrounded us and started asking Santiago for his money, I realized that they were completely ignoring my presence, as if I wasn't even there. In fact, one of the men was right against my body while Santiago was being robbed. I was completely immobile, unable to talk or even blink. I didn't feel any emotions; I was only observing the scene.

The men asked Santiago for his watch, but he couldn't react. So they pulled his watch off his wrist, scratching his skin. Then they turned away and left. At that moment, I was able to move and talk again. Feeling astonished I asked, "Santiago, are you okay? Your arm is bleeding."

He looked at me with his face still in shock and said, "I don't care about the watch or the money or my arm. None of that really matters. What really matters is what I have witnessed today. They didn't take anything from you because you were not here! This is something I cannot comprehend. This is completely out of my comprehension and my understanding."

"I don't know what happened either," I said. "Ever since I met you, incredible things have been occurring."

"All this is new to me. It is scary but also incredibly amazing. I think that I am going to stick with you!"

That day Santiago had witnessed the disappearance of my body from the eyes of the robbers. It was as if a cloak of invisibility and invulnerability had been placed upon me, not only making me not invisible to the robbers, but also taking all my fears away. According to Santiago, he could still see me, but then realized that my body wasn't really there when one of the men moved closer to him and was standing right where my body was. It was as if I was a hologram. At that moment Santiago became clearly aware that the three men were completely oblivious of my presence. How was this possible? We both wondered.

I couldn't wait to ask the Beings of Light about what had happened. Later that night they answered, "Sometimes extreme measures are required for the limited mind to get out of the way."

After knowing the Beings of Light for so many years I knew what they meant. "He is making himself ready for more. He is ready to expand, isn't he?"

"That's right. That is why you both met."

"Are extreme measures required for everyone?"

"Everyone is unique which makes every experience unique as well. Each person makes himself ready in his own way."

After this experience, Santiago and I became like brother and sister. His mind certainly became more open and he started to explore, learn, and use his own experiences, including his sufferings about his physical appearance — to teach and help others.

Dr. Ingrid Honkala, PhD

Ingrid is a Marine Biologist, Oceanographer, Master Scuba Diver, NASA and Navy Scientist, international lecturer, childhood near-death and spiritual transformative experiencer (NDEr and STEr). She has worked for the Colombian and US Navy for over thirteen years. Since birth, Ingrid lived and worked in intense combat zones of Colombia and was diagnosed with combat-related PTSD. Dr. Honkala has a great passion for understanding human consciousness and is helping to close the "gap of care" for people, especially children and combat soldiers, who have had NDEs and STEs. In her autobiography, "A Brightly Guided Life: How a Scientist Learned to Hear her Inner Wisdom," Ingrid details her amazing journey filled with all the challenges that brought her to reconnect with her inner-wisdom and to become a self-actualized and self-realized being.

Prelude to Lantern on the Beach

This next story is from my beloved brother Jeff, my partner in many childhood adventures.

Jeff would normally keep this kind of spiritual stuff to himself, as he is a strong bull in a china shop type of guy. One might describe him as a bit rough around the edges, but he is honest and full of love and care for all of us around him.

I admire his warm demeanor as he befriends everyone he meets, making a point to learn and remember their name. This was a lesson taught by the father we both adored and lost much too early in our lives. Our Father always felt it important to support local businesses, and to be a reliable courteous customer, and in turn you could expect to be treated fairly and honestly. Jeff has held onto this teaching, an adult man to man conversation, and one of the few he would ever have with him.

Our family recently needed a notary public for some legal paperwork, and I literally heard the theme song from 'Cheers' in my head as I watched him move about the bank with a big smile and open hand, greeting each and every member of the staff by name.

Jeff's biggest claim to fame is a love of fishing. He has earned the nickname 'fish whisperer' as not many have the talent of knowing the where and the why of the perfect spot they can be located, the perfect bait to entice any species of fish at any time of day, for any temperature of water, any fullness of the moon. He is well known by the park rangers all over the state, and I think that he once held an ambition to become one, until fate irrevocably changed his life those many years ago. Now he finds himself a partner of nature spending as much of his life outdoors as he possibly can, his skin maintaining a perfect glowing brown.

Jeff starts every year with a goal of catching a minimum of 1000 fish. Most will be a simple catch and release, though he keeps good eaters for himself and the neighbors. He has never fallen short of his goal in over 15 years, shattering his record this year with over 1,300 catches, giving each of them a name and a kiss before tossing them back into the depths. He keeps a log and accounting of his trips out and the resulting catches. Whether it's summer, fall, spring, or winter chopping through the ice, he can be found at the other end of a line somewhere.

And that is where this story begins....

THE LANTERN ON THE BEACH

By Jeffery Bud Watts

Strawberry Reservoir in the Utah mountains, is known for its cold deep waters and unpredictable weather. Wind and storms brew quickly, and the waters churn dark with foamy white caps. Of course, Jeff had the boat out on the water; it was the weekend and the cooler was full of beer, and he and his friend were catching.

There was not a lot of attention paid to the dark clouds that began to gather, and when the storm came, they decided it wasn't bad enough to quit early. So, they waited it out and laughed and drank until the winds calmed down and the rains stopped.

There was finally a realization that nightfall was quickly approaching, but the engine had stalled. They labored to get it started, but it was completely dark before they began to move. Cold and wet, they put the boat in full throttle and aimed it toward the dock.

With a sky full of clouds, the usual reflections of the moon and stars were not visible on the water. The boat's headlight gave little help as the two of them scanned the darkness ahead until finally spotting what they presumed was the dock, way off in the distance. They focused their attention there, and kept the engine pushing full speed ahead toward subtle flecks of light. They felt some relief as they inched closer to the warmth awaiting them in the truck parked close to the dock.

Neither of them had an inkling of the danger they faced. Neither of them identified land coming up as the engine roared behind them. But between them and the safety of the dock was an outlying cove and they were coming up to its beach in short order.

It was in those few moments before impact that Jeff saw something up ahead. Someone was standing on the shoreline swinging a lantern. He fixated on its light, close enough now to recognize it as a very old-style lantern. As it moved back and forth he heard a voice in his head, yelling to him, "STOP! LET UP! STOP! NOW!" He felt a recognition in both the voice and the un-seeable figure swinging the lantern directly ahead, and he let go of the throttle just seconds before hitting the beach.

Even as he was bounding threw the air from the force of the impact, he was thinking of the Dad he lost at fourteen and the many years of love and influence he had missed as he grew into manhood without him. Time seemed to stand still as his mind wrapped around the figure in the darkness, and the stern voice of a worried parent yelling "STOP!"

The old-time lantern had resembled the one that still hangs in the basement's furnace room near his dad's old camping gear, and the jar of the impact was less memorable than the feeling that his dad had just saved his life.

The boat's prop had dug deep into the sandy beach, bending into an unrecognizable blob of metal, but the two men would be able to walk away relatively unharmed.

As he got to his feet he called out "Thank you for helping us!" But his words fell into the otherwise silent air around him. He could no longer see the light, or the figure that had held it.

The boat was amazingly intact, but completely dug into the sand. His friend focused a flashlight on the beach as Jeff worked the boat backwards to the water. And as he labored he noticed that there were no footsteps in the sand other than his own.

As they slowly made their way to the safety of the dock, Jeff told him that he thought his dad had intervened and saved them. Although his friend neither accepted nor denied Jeff's feelings, Jeff was determined to find his own proof.

First of all, why would a stranger stand there waving a lantern to help them, and then not stick around a few extra moments to make sure they survived the impact? It just didn't make sense to him.

After docking the boat on the truck, he had to go back and look again. They followed the trail all the way to the deep crevasses made by their boat and bodies where they were forced to a sudden stop. The earlier rains had smoothed the sand along the trails headed toward the cove, and their flashlights revealed that the only footprints left there were their own.

There was no denying between them that someone had been on shore swinging a lantern to and fro, that each had witnessed a miracle on that beach, and that they had survived to tell the tale.

The effects of the beers had been replaced by an adrenaline rush, and they began to shiver and shake from the cold of wet clothes and the knowledge that 'someone or something' had shown up to save them. But for Jeff it was much more—it was an affirmation that he was not alone in this world, and it removed all doubt that the father he knew and loved was still with him, and always would be.

Jeff Watts, SLC Utah, as told to his sister, Claudia Watts Edge

HELP FROM THE TREE TOPS

By Marion Terry

The other day I sat on the back patio and watched my great-grandson awkwardly climb a small oak in our back yard. It was hard to just sit there and let him learn, but he had asked me to let him try by himself, and so I held myself back and silently prayed for his protection.

More and more confidently he would find his footing upward, and after a triumphant wave from the top, he began to climb back down. He ran up to me so proudly, thanking me for letting him do it all by himself, and I hugged him and told him I was proud of him too.

Later, as we sat on the big patio swing and slowly rocked together, he looked up at me and asked, "Who is Weo?" and I almost fell out of the swing. I asked him, "Why do you want to know?"

He answered me with the sweetest story of the nice man that was with him up in the tree, and he was telling him which branches to step on, and which ones were too little to hold him. He said the man told him "You be careful climbing trees, and if you ever get in trouble, just call out my name" and so he asked him what his name was and he answered, "I have many names, but you can just call me Weo."

That evening we had a long talk, and I told him that the man in the tree was my daddy and his great granddaddy. I explained that when his Uncle Matthew was a little boy, he could never say "granddaddy," and that it always came out "Weo." So his mother and uncle started calling him this nickname, like our grand-kids call their granddaddy AdDad.

We spent a great deal of time together as I told my grandson all about my daddy and the fabulous things he did in his lifetime, and when I showed him his picture, he enthusiastically pointed to it and said "YES! That's Weo!" My heart skipped a beat, actually several beats, because I knew for absolute certainty that my Daddy had been with us, and that he is still looking out for all of us.

Marion Terry, Lake Wales, Florida

Chapter Six

SPONTANEOUS AWARENESS

Rebecca Austill-Clausen MS, OTR,/L, FAOTA	THE JOY OF OPENING MY HEART
Jesse Warren Clayton	GOODBYE FOR NOW A Hunter's Moment of Spiritual Enlightenment
Steve Marr	EVEN IN DEATH HE WAS WORRIED ABOUT HIS DRY CLEANING (the in-between Heaven and Earth)

THE JOY OF OPENING MY HEART

By Rebecca Austill-Clausen

My 37-year-old brother David passed in 1995 after a seven-year battle with AIDS.

Three years before he transitioned, David and I walked on the sandy, wind-swept Coast Guard Beach at the National Seashore on Cape Cod, Massachusetts. We were enjoying our traditional summer camping reunion with our family and friends. Evening happy hours fill with food, drinks, frivolity, and music from our 18 wooded campsites. Each day began with a morning dip in the clear, calm glacier-formed kettle pond surrounding our campgrounds. After breakfast, we changed into dry swimsuits and bundled our colorful beach umbrellas, towels, and lobster rolls into the back of our cars, and drove to the ocean. David lived in Newburyport, Massachusetts. I lived in Pennsylvania, so we were thrilled to be together for a glorious two weeks of summer fun.

It was at a time when we heard daily news shouting that thousands of people were dying from AIDS. There were no survivors once someone was diagnosed with this deadly disease. People had no idea what caused AIDS except that it seemed to be decimating men who were gay. David told his family and friends that he was gay when he was in his early 20s and I casually asked if he had been tested for AIDS.

David turned away and did not immediately answer. The sun quickly disappeared behind dense gray clouds. My heart began to pound an irregular rhythm of fear and disbelief that escalated as the seconds ticked away. What was David going to say? He was four years younger than me, and we were extremely close. Waiting for his answer was the longest ten seconds of my life. David finally turned towards me, hesitating as he looked me in the eye and said, "I am HIV positive. I had no idea what HIV positive was and asked what it meant. "HIV turns into AIDS," he said. My heart stopped beating. My mind begins to race as I quickly ask about his medical care. My brother is going to die? My heart screams in terror and disbelief. None of this makes sense. What can I do? How can I help? My brother can't die!

David calmly states that he has received the best medical care from the most skilled AIDS specialist in Boston for the past four years. I am stunned. Most people with AIDS were dying within three years. He has already survived with an HIV positive diagnosis for four years. David says he doesn't want to be treated any differently and he clearly emphasizes that he is taking all the precautions, especially when around our preschool age sons, Ken and Ryan. He asks me not to tell anyone, including my husband, Jeff. I immediately agree. I will do anything for my brother. I didn't realize, though, that I now have no support system by not being able to share David's condition.

After returning home, I find myself in the New Age section of our local Barnes and Noble bookstore. I am a science-based Occupational Therapist. I have no idea what New Age means, but I realize now that I was directed to this area by my spirit guides. I find myself looking at books about the afterlife. I grew up as a PK – a Preacher's Kid. My Dad's an Episcopalian minister, yet I don't recall ever talking about the afterlife. I thought we lived on Earth, and then we died. I had no idea there could be life after death.

I begin reading dozens and then hundreds of books about the afterlife during the three years after David confidentially told me he had AIDS. It was important to me that authors writing about the afterlife appear "normal." Later I become aware that I was spiritually directed to authors that would resonate with me. I am a voracious reader and read everything written beginning with my chosen author's first book. I want to understand the author's journey from the start. I shared some of these books with David, particularly those by Mary Summer Rain, so when he passed, we were both aware that maybe there was an afterlife. Yet, neither of us knew anyone who believed there was life after death.

David passed on October 1, 1995, after a seven-year battle with AIDS. He was considered a long-term survivor of this horrendous disease.

When my brother transitioned 25 years ago, I was filled with despair. My heart was closed to everything except intense grief. I believed all life events can be positive, but I could find nothing positive about David's death. Yet, on the day described below, I opened my heart and received the best Christmas present of my Earthly existence. I'd like to share an excerpt from my book, "Change Maker, How My Brothers' Death Woke Up My Life."

"About eight weeks after my brother David passed, my horse Astre and I were ambling through the woods on a crisp fall morning following our favorite forest trail, which meandered through a Christmas tree farm.

I slowly breathed in the sharp scent of winter frost. My eyes crinkled with delight at dozens of bare oak trees, their branches lined with hundreds of sparkling white icicles that cast miniature rainbows across our trail. My heart felt wide open. I was filled with joy and sang out, "Thank you, universe, for such a glorious day!"

Astre and I seemed to be all alone as we reached the center of the Christmas tree pasture. I closed my eyes in contentment.

Three feet in front of me, standing on a light-green grassy knoll, stood David!

I immediately noticed he was healthy. He looked about thirty years old and was wearing jeans, sandals, and a red-and-black plaid flannel shirt. His big, beautiful brown eyes looked directly into my soul. He smiled broadly. My eyes remained closed.

"David!" I felt questions burst from my mouth. "How are you? It's great to see you! What are you doing here? How are you feeling?"

David grinned and answered telepathically, a phenomenon I later learned was called thought transference.

I realized speech was unnecessary: Sending messages via stream of consciousness, or "thought," was much faster than speaking with words. I sent my questions telepathically and received instantaneous answers. I shared my extreme sadness at his death, my halfhearted attempts to focus on work, my inability to understand the purpose of his passing. I absorbed his rapid-fire responses: his acceptance of the situation, his willingness to communicate, his ability to transmit unconditional love. Then we shared family updates.

I soaked up his presence and bloomed like a wilted flower returning to life. Within seconds, we had communicated all our feelings and emotions surrounding his passing. We were flushed with joy and laughter, thrilled to be together again!

This was absolutely the best thing that could have happened to me, unless David were still alive in this physical realm. A brilliant blue sky glistened with a thousand beams of sunlight surrounding us; rays of joy penetrated my bereaved soul. I was ecstatic to be with my brother.

I looked beyond David and was flabbergasted to see dozens of people. They stood in a relaxed, semi-straight line that stretched horizontally across the right side of the same hill where David was standing. I looked more closely and realized they were the most cherished people in my life who had passed from Earth.

Closest were my maternal grandparents, Grandma and Grandpa Dole, holding hands as always. Grandpa and Grandma had always been together, and here they were again, sharing their love with me as I stared in amazement!

To their right was our dear childhood friend Edward. His lanky frame towered over Grandma and Grandpa, and his huge smile beamed at me. I grinned back, remembering the times we shared together. He was a wonderful friend who passed away about 6 months before David.

Beside Edward was my dear friend Holly. She had passed away suddenly in her early twenties, killed in a car accident. During my freshman year of college, Holly asked me to be her Installing Officer when she was elected to be Worthy Advisor in the Order of the Rainbow Girls, a charitable Masonic organization I belonged to in my teens. When I had been Worthy Advisor several years before, I had thoroughly enjoyed the leadership role. But as much as I wanted to help Holly, I didn't have the time to devote to memorizing the installing script. I had to tell her I couldn't do the job, even though I felt awful about refusing her request.

But now Holly and I smiled, delighted to be together. She held no judgment about me. All my guilt, held in for over twenty years, immediately dissipated.

Enveloped by love, I stared at the peaceful gathering that extended across the hillside. I had totally forgotten about Astre, who stood quietly underneath me, not moving. I returned my attention to David, who continued to grin widely.

I thought my heart would burst with exuberance and joy, and I laughed like a child who had just discovered the magic of ice cream for the first time.

I beamed as I started to realize the implications of David's still being alive. The concept of life continuing forever was mindboggling. I could actually see him, talk with him, and share my feelings and love. My soul trilled with happiness. I felt like a huge display of fireworks had just erupted. A crescendo of magic, sound, excitement, and pleasure radiated through me.

Beyond the gathered friends was a bright gold arch about seven feet tall. In many of the metaphysical books I'd read, visualizing an arch or a doorway typically symbolizes a passageway to another realm. I expected David to walk me under the arch, but instead my diminutive Grandma Dole took me by the hand, and we skipped underneath together.

The sky turned bright fuchsia immediately after we passed under the arch. "Get oooo-ver here," shouted Gramps (my Dad's father), his big booming voice filled with glee. I did not see Gramps, but I clearly heard his voice. He took my hand into his own sturdy palm. I felt myself lift off the ground, and we flew through the gorgeous fuchsia sky, leaving David and our other friends behind. All sense of time had ceased to exist; it seemed like we flew for hours. We reminisced telepathically, and I sparkled with joy.

All of a sudden, Astre moved, her feet gently clip-clopping on the snow-covered ground. My body, perched on her firm back, began to sway gently.

"Gramps, I need to get back!" We made a wide banking turn back the way we'd come.

"I will always be here," Gramps said reassuringly as the glowing arch appeared again.

I zipped through the arch and arrived at the same place where I'd begun this journey. David, Grandma and Grandpa, Edward, Holly, and all the others were in the same positions on the hill. I could feel Astre's gait begin to pick up, and I called out, "I need to go back! Will you be here again?" I heard a resounding chorus: "Yes! We will always be here!"

I opened my eyes and pulled back the reins to stop Astre's movement.

Wow—what an incredible experience! I laughed ecstatically.

David is alive! My grandparents are still alive! Edward and Holly have returned!

Life is eternal!

I sat on Astre's back in the Christmas tree farm for a long time, thinking about life, death, and the afterlife. Even though I'm a preacher's kid, I had never spent time thinking much about eternity before.

I stared at my watch—only twenty minutes had passed since I'd closed my eyes, seen these beloved people, and flown with Gramps through the brilliant sky. But it felt like I'd been gone for hours. Those twenty minutes had changed my entire understanding of life. My brain whirled. If life was eternal, it meant I didn't need to rush around so much, trying to accomplish all my goals and dreams in this lifetime.

If we live forever, Earth is just one of many places we experience. I tingled with excitement. Eternity was a long time! I had no doubt that David, friends, relatives, and people I didn't even know who had passed on were alive; they just lived in a different dimension. I had never understood the purpose of life, but I was filled with a new purpose of my own: I wanted to learn how to communicate with them.

None of the hundreds of metaphysical and new age books I had read since learning about David's HIV diagnosis included experiences identical to mine, but they all described spiritual transformation. I knew it was time for me to find a teacher—someone I could question who could be my mentor and my spiritual guide. But where did I need to look? How could I find someone to teach me something I could barely describe? (Austill-Clausen, 2016, pp. 40-44).

I looked for a teacher and found a shaman. Change Maker describes my multiple Spiritual Transformative Experiences with the afterlife during the first year following David's passage. I learned how to continue communicating with David and hundreds of spiritual entities. I discovered automatic writing and now have over two thousand pages of life-affirming, heart-centered channeled information ready to share. I became a Reiki Master and found that Reiki enhances afterlife communication. I studied shamanic journeying, meditation, crystal energy, sound healing, and forest bathing, and I became a spiritual coach. I now realize that the hundreds of books I read before David passed opened my mind to receive and communicate with him and with my other deceased loved ones in the Christmas tree farm.

For 20 years I struggled with how my spiritual awakening could mesh with the everyday world. Finally I gained the courage to publish 'Change Maker, How My Brother's Death Woke Up My Life.' But first, I sold my 32-year-old rehabilitation business that I started myself and included close to 400 staff and 13,000 clients a year. I sold this labor of love to my Chief Financial Officer before Change Maker was published. I didn't think it was a good idea for people to know that their "boss" talked with dead people!

I published Change Maker with She Writes Press, and with some trepidation. I wondered if I would be professionally ostracized. The book reviews were outstanding. I've been thrilled and frankly flabbergasted as Change Maker, illustrated by Micki McAllister, has now won five national book awards. Change Maker is filled with hundreds of books and resources, organized for each chapter, and designed for people that want to awaken to a world beyond. Each chapter ends with an "Illumination" – guidance, suggestions, encouragement, and inspiration for readers who wish to pursue their own spiritual journey. Change Maker begins in October, the month David passes, and ends in July with a spectacular afterlife affirming event.

In the five years since Change Maker was published, I have shared my afterlife journey with thousands of people worldwide. I love public speaking and watching the lightbulbs go off in people's minds as they realize what happened to me is possible for anyone. I teach After-Death Communication workshops and a 7-week LIVE online After-Death Communication program. An After-Death Communication course survey provided at the end of the 7-week course showed that 100% of the people that completed the survey believe they can receive and share after-death communication with their deceased loved ones. The afterlife is real.

I'm delighted to be the first person to teach courses in Reiki, a natural healing energy modality, at the American Occupational Therapy Association Annual Conference for the past five years. I also teach one-day Reiki courses at multiple medical universities, and at national and state conferences nationwide and online. Reiki enhances afterlife communication.

The question of eternal life has captured imaginations forever. We wonder if Earthbound existence is all there is. If there is more, what form does "more" take? Our biological scientific society eliminates communication from life beyond the veil as an impossible fantasy. Yet millions of people who have had Near-Death Experiences or Spiritual Transformative Experiences return to Earthly life with an unshakable belief in the existence of an afterlife.

The International Association for Near-Death Studies (IANDS.org), a worldwide community of professional educators, researchers, and experiencers, has explored the existence of life after death for 40 years. IANDS has just reached a fantastic milestone in collaboration with John Hopkins University Press to publish personal stories that substantiate life's existence beyond Earthly reality. This information will be disseminated free of charge to health care professionals to serve as a discussion-teaching guide. I enjoy the camaraderie and sophistication of the IANDs community immensely.

I sincerely appreciate the opportunity to share my afterlife adventures with Claudia Watts Edge in this fantastic book, "We Touched Heaven." Thank you, Claudia, from the center of my heart and soul for including me in your delightful compilation of stories about the afterlife.

Rebecca Austill, Clausen, Downingtown, Pennsylvania

MS, OTR/L, FAOTA, Award-Winning Author: *Change Maker, How My Brother's Death Woke Up My Life*

Reiki Master, Speaker, Occupational Therapist
President, Complementary Health Works

To sign up for Rebecca's newsletter, register for her online programs, schedule a free Discovery coaching session, or submit requests to speak, please feel free to contact Rebecca via her website:

https://RebeccaAustillClausen.com or email:
becky@RebeccaAustillClausen.com

GOODBYE FOR NOW

A Hunter's Moment of Spiritual Enlightenment

By Jesse Warren Clayton

October 8, 2016, I remember this day, I had looked forward to hunting with my son-in-law, Marcos. He was a newer hunter with an Elk permit and I would enjoy teaching him what I had learned in my years of exploring nature. Deep into the back country, communication with the rest of the world is severed, and after a few days under the stars, you can feel yourself morph and change. The body begins to recuperate from the permeating noise that we allow ourselves to grow accustomed too in the world below the mountains.

You begin to really hear again. I listen to the birds overhead and note that they will tell you a story about what is happening over a mile away. Your sense of smell also becomes super sensitive. Each variety of vegetation and its underbrush has its own scent, and the animal that beds in it takes on its aroma. Elk has a sweet heady musk, and a deer is tangy sage. Even water has a smell of its own and I can recognize it from miles away.

The wind has distinct currents that feel like Earth's breath as it inhales, making it harder to climb upwards. And you can feel it exhale against the back of your neck. The Catawba Indian blood that has been strained and diluted over several generations rises and swells within my veins, and I become re-acquainted with the sound of my own heartbeat. I am alive out here, and this is what I wish to teach my son.

We have saved up workdays off, collecting them to go off into the wilderness without a clock or a calendar. It takes months of careful planning and many weekends prior to the hunt watching for traces of them, learning their habits, the trails where they walk, feed, and bed down. All of our planning had cumulated to this point in time, as we lay deep in the brush and silently wait.

I want to add a caveat here before I get too deep into my story. I do not hunt for sport. I do not kill for gratification, for trophies, or smiling selfies. I love and respect all life, especially the animal I am hunting. I provide for my family, and I am glad that I know how, should things ever shut down and food become hard to get. A long time ago, I made the decision that I would not fight other families for the last bit of food on a shelf. I have lived my life as a provider, and if I know how to hunt, I can also help provide for others too. I hunt in respect for the life of the animal and none of it goes to waste. It is important, and I want Marcos to learn this too.

A hunting day starts early, and it is dark and cold as we set up an hour before sunrise on the ridge above our camp. The dew is just beginning to form as the moisture in the air gets heavy, leaving droplets all around us. We lay in complete stillness, each wispy ghost-like breath building ice crystals in our beards and eyebrows. The body begs for the sun to come up, and as it begins to rise over the ridges, you watch the line between the light and receding shadow move ever closer to you with bated anticipation. The animal wants to shed the dew too, and the moment the warmth of the sunlight hits their body, they shift into the open and start to move.

Sure enough, only a few minutes into the morning and the elk are already routing around. I know the area, I have walked it for months prior to this day. I know by my studying that this is the best time to spot them, just as the sun comes up. And I have no doubt that we will see them today.

We are in a great spot, although a bit further from them than I would have liked. As we heard them advancing toward us, I was excited for Marcos to see them up close, and we motioned to each other, deciding to take the shot. We waited until the lead cow had reached the middle of a small clearing about 400 yards directly in front of us. Marcos fired, and I backed him up with a shot of my own.

She is hit, but it is not a perfect shot. She is badly wounded and still trying to get away from her invisible assailants. I fire another shot, but something is wrong. My scope has moved, and no shot I fire now will be accurate. Marcos fired the last of his three shots but missed, although the shot was close enough to keep her from darting deeper into the undergrowth. Unsure where to run, she sits down behind some brush.

We needed to get to her fast, but she is on a steep slope, and it will take a while for us to reach her. Marcos is younger and faster, and bounds down the mountain to find her, while I continue to fire shots above her so she will hold still.

I knew she is scared, and I did not want her to suffer. As Marcos got closer, I picked my own way down to get to her. She was on the steepest side of the mountain, hidden in deep deadfall and thick, overgrown bush, making it impossible to find any landmarks in the route I had chosen. It was a steep slope, and I was mentally preparing myself for the hard climb back up the other side. By choosing to split up, we could cover a lot more ground in a race to find her. We knew she was in there somewhere.

I caught her scent and called out to Marcos while pointing for him to head my way.

And then I saw her, just six feet away and staring at me, eye to eye. She did not jump or run; she didn't make a sound. She was watching me, staring into me, and her thoughts penetrated deep into my very soul. I seemed to have stepped out of my own awareness, and I knew she had stepped out too. I could actually feel her experiencing me and my concerns for her.

We were each other at that exact moment in time. Our feelings had somehow become intertwined and she knew my true intent. And we both understood what would have to happen next. It is hard to explain, but I could hear her as she spoke directly into me. She told me it was OK, she was ready now. And in those moments, I understood how connected all of us really are, in both this life and the next. I understood that I would see her again and that I would also BE her again, as a forever connection.

As my son moved closer, I took a deep breath. I raised my rifle and shot. She died almost instantly, and as she gracefully laid down her head, I watched her soul leave through the windows of her eyes.

I don't feel this experience was negative in any way. We had shared love, a commonality, and a connection that was bigger than both of us. It was a lesson we learned together, and we knew that both of our souls would grow from this experience.

I know that I will never forget her. I offer my eternal love and gratitude for her and for our shared experience. I give the body she leaves behind my respect and gratitude for what it will provide, and I say sincerely "Goodbye for now."

Jesse Warren Clayton, Kearns, Utah

Permitted hunting is a careful accounting of the numbers of herds of deer and elk by the fish and game/wildlife departments, and is an act of preservation and survival for all life in the region. it is necessary to help keep the population strong and with enough vegetation to provide food, least the herds spend winters suffering starvation and disease.

EVEN IN DEATH HE WAS STILL WORRIED ABOUT HIS DRY CLEANING

My story is not an NDE (near-death experience), but it has similarities!

By Steve Marr

I am now 65 years old, and this "dream" occurred when I was 32. I had gone to bed at 10pm as usual one night, only to abruptly awaken just before midnight. I could feel my body indicating a digestive system purge, and I quickly proceeded to the toilet. I could feel the energy around me change and I become chilled with my hair standing on end. The thought that entered my mind was, "oh boy, what's happening tonight that I have had a forced purge?" I return to my bed, lay down my head, and promptly enter into a "dream."

I am sitting on a chair in a darkish "room" when a child comes up behind me and begins to run his fingers through my long hair. At first I ignore him, but he repeats the procedure until I swiftly turn to him and enquire as to why he has not hidden himself from me, for I know that he is a spirit.

As he tells me his name, age (13yrs) and what he had died of, an older man waits in the deeper shadows for us. The boy informs me that they had been instructed to show me where we go immediately after death, and to follow him.

As we pass the older man, he greets me and asks if I remember him, which I did. I answered that he was our family funeral insurance broker who had died five months prior to that. He tells me to let my parents know that he is happy where he is.

I then accompany them to a doorway with the brightest white light streaming from it, and I enter into what I can only describe as a huge "auditorium" with thousands of "balls" of differently colored lights flitting all over.

The lights have no race, gender, or religion. The happiness and love they display there are indescribable.

On my entry, recognizing that I am from the "physical world" some lights start rushing excitedly to me. They take on form to relate who they were when they had died and what they had died of.

One man asks of me to fetch his pants at a dry-cleaning business, as he was not able to collect them. The spirits around us laugh as they relay that he refuses to accept that he is no longer in need of his material things after his death. He had been run over and killed in a motor accident soon after taking the pants in to the dry cleaners, and he was having a hard time accepting being dead.

I then enquire after my late brother's and uncle's whereabouts, and I am told that this area is only for those of recent deaths. From here they will learn to proceed to the higher levels where the longer deceased are. Those on the higher levels can freely visit the lower ones, but the newly deceased have to "learn" to rise.

I tell the spirits around me this is the most wonderful experience to be shown these things, as I have always questioned what happens after death. I am then told it is time for me to leave and I am taken to a different door. I am instructed that because I am from the physical world, that I have to return via this door, whereas they cannot.

I thank them for having shown me such wonders, and I exit though the door. I immediately woke up in my bed thinking, "Wow, what a wonderful experience I had just had!"

I do not believe that it was a dream, and I always relate this experience to those I encounter who fear dying!

Steve Marr, Cape Town, South Africa

Steve's story reminds me very much of the Astral Plane I have written about in my previous books. As Steve stated, the place he was shown was of the dimension closest to earth's physical life. It is here that newly passed souls, or confused souls reside while they are trying to get used to their new surroundings and the idea that they have passed into a new form of being.

Their bodies are gone, but their thoughts and actions can still render a longing towards the physical. The boy who stroked Steve's hair is most likely only a mischievous child who is looking for attention through the living, as are most ghostly experiences. Eventually these souls will look to the light or to the beings who were described by Steve, as they are there to help them find it.

Chapter Seven

THE WISDOM OF CHILDREN

Whatever you're doing today,

Do it with the confidence

Of a four-year-old

In a batman t-shirt

Ifunny.com

I SAW YOU FROM UP THERE

By Chelsea Rose Clayton

"**M**om, remember when you used to smoke cigarettes like dad?"

I was driving when my five-year-old daughter Harper posed this question, and I had to pause a moment before responding. I had to think backward to the last time that smoking was even a part of my routine. I had quit entirely many years before pregnancy and bringing my curious twins into the world.

Just in case I hadn't heard her the first time, she repeated the question, and so I went into an explanation that I had not smoked since long before she was born.

Without missing a beat, she interrupted me, saying "Oh yah, that was when I saw you from up there. The statement was so innocent, as if she were just remembering something completely natural.

I have heard it said that we choose our parents before being born. Could it really be that she was shown and picked me to be her Mother? Are we together in the here and now because of our choices, because I am sure that I definitely picked her right back.

Chelsea Rose Clayton, SLC. Utah

Speak to your Children
as if they are the Wisest,
Kindest,
most Beautiful,
and Magical Humans on Earth,
for what they Believe
is what they will Become.

Author unknown

I DON'T REMEMBER HEAVEN
ANYMORE GRANDMA

This morning as I sat with a second cup of coffee, my four-year old granddaughter Harper leaned in close to me with a serious look on her face and whispered "Grandma, I don't remember Heaven anymore." It was a profound statement, and as I fumbled for a response, she added "I used to be able to see it whenever I wanted to, but now when I try, well, I just can't see it."

I am so happy to have found the patience that eluded me as a young mother of five. I'm sure that if I had been able to slow down and listen in between cooking meals, brushing teeth and evening baths, they were probably trying to tell me their own amazing discoveries, and I lament what I missed in those busy days.

My pace is much slower now, allowing me to be completely present with the children they have brought into the world, and I appreciate the special bonds of trust and the conversations that arise from the depths of their hearts.

In this extraordinary moment with Harper, the best response I could offer was a big Grandma hug as I wrapped my arms tightly around her, and whispered my own secret longing, "I sure wish I could remember it too."

Claudia Watts Edge

SOMETIMES I WONDER

by Brownell Landrum

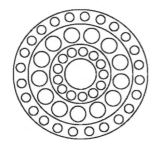

Sometimes I Wonder
If this isn't home
And I don't mean Paris
or London or Rome

A place where I came from
And will go again
A world so mysterious
It makes my head spin

This world is all magic
And a glow that's so bright
When I squeeze my eyes shut
I can still feel the light

Some call it Heaven
Some Paradise
To me it's a party
Where everyone's nice

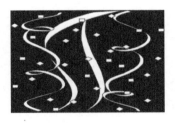

We'll have friends who'll be there
With warm open hands
And music to greet us
Like grand marching bands

It's the place where we plan
Who we'll be with and when
We pick out our names
Like Sara and Ben

Or Williams, Rodriguez
Ivanov or Chen
Whoever we choose
Will feel like our kin

We decide our lessons
The paths we will take
Awards we might go for
And mistakes we might make

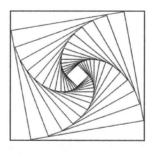

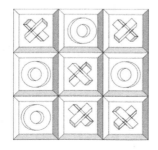

For life isn't easy
And not always fun
But easy is boring
Like games always won

So we set up our challenges
And mountains so high
To test our endurance
And reach for the sky

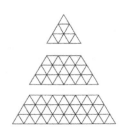

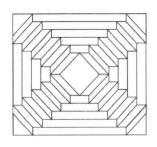

It doesn't much matter
If we get to the top
What matters much more
Is what we do when we stop

Do we smell the roses?
Admire the bees?
Enjoy the sensation
of a warm ocean breeze?

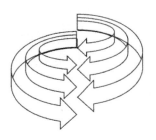

Or do we stew and fuss
And blame someone else
Instead of taking a look
Back into our self?

Do we ask for help?
And give in return?
Its best when we realize
There's a lesson to learn

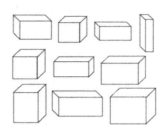

A wise man once said
What matters in the end
Does the love you receive
Match the love you spend?

I have one piece of wisdom
For a smart kid like you
Advice I hope you'll hear
And realize its true

Abandon all jealousy
Anger and greed
And open your heart
To people in need

Give yourself freely

With no fear and no doubt

And then you'll be proud

Of how you turned out

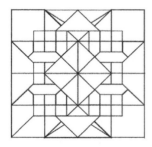

So when you're back home

And see your old friends

All will sing and rejoice

And cheer in the end

Brownell Landrum

Sometimes I Wonder is a one in a series of Wonderactive Books by Brownell Landrum. Check out Brownell's other books and projects at BrownellLandrum.com or on Amazon.

Brownell Landrum

Writer, Speaker, Inventor, Marketer, Innovator

Brownell is such a talented writer, and generously put several of her thought-provoking children's books at my disposal. I wish I had more room to include them here, but please visit her website brownelllandrum.com.

And for a charming way to handle the subject of reincarnation with a child check out her book, 'THIS ISN'T MY FIRST TIME'.

FIRST GRADE FOR ME MEANT PEARL HARBOR, DEATH, SENSORY MIXUPS

By PMH Atwater, LHD

War was in your lap when bombs dropped on Pearl Harbor. Everyday real. Everywhere present. Any cans you emptied to prepare a meal, you washed, flattened, then set aside in a box to take once a week to the drop-off place where the metal was collected by the Army to use in the war effort. There were Victory Gardens. If you didn't grow your own food you didn't eat much. Going to the grocery store meant taking the food you raised with you so you could can it at the store. Literally, grocery stores were canning kitchens. You paid for metal used at check out, plus anything you could grab from near-empty food shelves. So much was rationed: butter, gasoline, blankets, sugar. Maybe more, but I don't remember the rest. And air-raid drills. Wailing sirens meant lights out. Wardens checked every home, barged right in. You were fined if they found anything, like a cigarette still glowing. We got through this by helping each other. If you had extra food, you'd put it in a paper bag, set it on your neighbor's porch, ring the doorbell and run. People were proud. You didn't want to embarrass anyone.

I started school a little early, not quite six. Washington School was a long walk from where I lived in Twin Falls, Idaho. That walk haunted me for decades. . because.... . it was a walk of death.

In those days, if anyone in your family paid the ultimate price in the war effort, you were sent a large gold star decal from the government that you put in your living room window — so everyone would know what had happened to one of your own. It seemed to me like those gold stars popped up everywhere. Kids know what's going on. I knew those gold stars were death stars, and my walk to school was a walk with their death call. One morning, there were six new gold stars on the window of a home I passed. I just stood there and sobbed. I don't recall a single morning in all of first grade, when I didn't have to stop my tears and shudders just to walk in the door of my first-grade classroom.

But that wasn't all. When I entered my school room, punishment greeted me. That's because I was the only kid in my first-grade class who could smell color, see music, and hear numbers. (This sensory extra is called synesthesia or multiple sensing and is an elaboration of the limbic system in the brain.) Who knew anything about what most assuredly must be some form of nonsense? Certainly not the teachers and principal in my school. It was enough that I was born with dyslexia. Reading was difficult, words danced around, and letters sometimes changed places. Kids would laugh every time I tried to read out loud. I dreaded such exercises. Took me three years to teach myself how to read. No one else helped. Invented all the "how-tos" I needed by sensing what felt right, then drilling myself hour after hour with comic books and Sunday funnies, matching what I saw with what I said, sneaking in time so no one could guess what I was doing in the "milk house" near the barn. This anomaly shows up today only if get too tired or don't feel well. The three years of "whenever-I-could-practice" paid off. But my sensing differences, the synesthesia, formed a mountain almost too tall to climb.

A kid who could smell color, see music, and hear numbers was beyond the pale. The principal of my school called my mother in twice, trying to get her to allow him to commit me to a special school for "congenital liars." She refused to cooperate, yet for years afterward she questioned the wisdom of her decision. As for the principal, he made certain my first-grade teacher had me sit on a tall stool in front of the class as an example of a bad child who told lies. Many times when this occurred I also had to wear a tall conical hat that said "DUNCE" on it. I knew I was telling the truth, but everyone else thought I was lying. The result? Utter confusion. Truth branded me a liar; people turned on me. Lies, on the other hand, pleased everyone while confusing me.

By the end of the first grade, I was so angry I decided that I would never become an adult when I grew up because all adults were stupid. This anger fueled an almost obsessive need on my part to cross-check almost everything and everyone. What teachers and most adults told me, I rejected. I cross-compared and studied every little thing to find out why my world was so different from everyone else's. And I carefully observed how people walked, what they wore, how they spoke, who they were with and when, to see if I could learn anything from their traits that might help me with mine. Quickly I nixed what people said — as few if any said what they meant. Instead I watched what they actually did and what effect that had — like throwing pebbles in a lake: it's not the pebble that matters, it's all those ripples, what they are and where they go. I claim no wisdom here. Just the pain of trial and error.

The anger I felt from my first-grade debacle mixed with a deep horror. Pearl Harbor, World War II, Hitler, Nazi "goose-steppers" all melded into a daily fare that was triggered for me by those gold stars. For years afterwards, I did everything I could to avoid getting a score of 100% on school papers. If I did, that meant I would be "awarded" a gold star: translate - "death star." I could not tolerate any form of gold until I was in my fifties, could not wear gold or anything gold colored until I was in my sixties. That long.

So here we are with Covid-19 and it's like Pearl Harbor all over again. Scenes of death have mixed with that first year in grade school when I tried to be like everyone else and failed, utterly. Being confined to my home now has been an eye-opener. For 44 years I have been researching near-death states, with a research base now of nearly 5,000 adult/child experiencers, wrote 18 books related to or about the subject, not counting six children's books called the Animal Lights Series, to help parents with early memories of their children. Certainly, I was told to do all of this by what I call The Voice Like None Other, which spoke to me during my third death/near-death experience. No arguing that point. Yet, in looking around me, hearing and feeling what today's people are experiencing, it seems to me as if a re-run of my earliest years.

I was born in Twin Falls, Idaho, and I died in Boise, Idaho. What I have accomplished as a near-death researcher only mimics that little first grader with learning differences who death once stalked.

PMH Atwater, LHD

PMH is an international authority on near-death states, PMH Atwater is the author of 19 books, her writings have also appeared in numerous magazines and newspapers. She has lectured twice at the United Nations and guested on tv and radio talk shows such as Sally Jessy Raphael, Larry King Live, Entertainment Tonight, Regis & Kathy Lee, Geraldo, and The Shirley Show in Canada. Recently she was awarded the "Lifetime Achievement

Award" from the National Association of Transpersonal Hypnotherapists and the "Outstanding Service Award" from IANDS (where she has also been a 2 term board member).

"Some say you are too painful to remember. I say you are too precious to forget." "I held you every second of your life." "Heaven and earth may separate us today, but nothing will ever change the fact that you made me a mom."

Author Unknown

Chapter Eight

THE LOSS OF A CHILD

MORGAN'S STORY

A Gift of Love from Mt. Everest

By Elizabeth Boisson

On October 20th, 2009, my son Morgan James Pierre Boisson passed of severe altitude sickness at the Base Camp of Mount Everest in Tibet. It was the most devastating day of my life but at the same time it was the moment I realized that love never dies.

I was able to speak to his roommate by cell phone and asked him to put it to Morgan's ear. He had stopped breathing and was undergoing CPR. I told Morgan that we loved him, not to be afraid, and that we were very proud of him. At the exact instant Morgan stopped breathing, I felt him with me. It was a warm, calming feeling that washed through me and was hugging me from the inside. I realized that he was comforting me and that he wanted me to know that he would always be with me. I knew in an instant that love never dies.

Before Morgan died, I did not believe it would be possible to carry on without one of my children. However, I realized that I had to carry on, not only for my two daughters who needed me, but more importantly for Morgan, whose only wish is to see us happy. I knew we had to live and thrive for him.

My strongest desire after his death was to somehow communicate with him. I didn't know how this would be possible—I had never been to a psychic medium, but Morgan took matters into his own hands.

I had been practicing yoga at a studio for years, and Morgan had sometimes gone with me. Angie Bayliss, the owner of the studio, decided in November 2009 to interview a psychic medium who had recently moved to the area looking for rental space. Angie's way of evaluating the psychic medium, Susanne Wilson, was to ask Susanne to 'read' a photo of my kids included in our annual Christmas card. She provided no other information to Susanne.

Susanne connected with my son, communicating his personality and mannerisms. Susanne gave Angie numerous validations including details that were not public knowledge and not known to Angie (who diligently wrote everything down). I will share a few highlights. Susanne said a young man showed her a big teddy bear and bottle of Captain Morgan. My son's name is Morgan and we affectionately call him Big Bear. He is also nicknamed "Captain." Susanne saw him shouting through a megaphone that he was OKAY— very significant because Morgan was a cheerleader at the University of Arizona and his megaphone was at his memorial service.

Susanne saw him on a mountain, lying on his back. She saw a black box at his ear; that he had listened intently but had been unable to speak. He told Susanne to say, "Mom, I heard everything you said, and I love you back." It was wonderful to know Morgan had heard me when the phone was held to his ear.

Susanne further told Angie that my son and his two roommates were like a "band of brothers." Although Morgan was close to all the students who helplessly watched him die that morning, his two roommates were especially important to him. Colin and Matt accompanied Morgan's body to Lhasa and waited with him until my husband was able to finally get a visa to enter Tibet six days later.

Perhaps the most amazing fact was that Susanne told Angie that we would receive a special rock from the place that Morgan died, and she sketched the rock, that was split in two halves. We made no mention of this detail to anyone. A month later Morgan's roommate Colin delivered Morgan's rock upon his return from China, just as Susanne had described.

I had my own reading with Susanne in which more validations came through, including that Morgan and I would work together to help parents connect with their deceased children in the afterlife. I founded my parents support group one month later. Susanne also introduced me to Mark Ireland, whose son Brandon also passed on a mountain, and we later co-founded Helping Parents Heal in March of 2012.

Morgan continues to work diligently in the Spirit world to help children get messages through to their parents, and I am incredibly proud of him. Love never dies.

Elizabeth Boisson

President & Co-Founder, Helping Parents Heal, Inc., Newsletter Editor. Two of Elizabeth's children have transitioned; her daughter, Chelsea, in 1991 and her son, Morgan, in 2009 from severe altitude sickness while on a student trip to the Base Camp of Mt Everest in Tibet. Immediately after, Elizabeth created the Facebook group Parents United in Loss. Then in 2012 she joined forces with Mark Ireland to form Helping Parents Heal. Elizabeth is a certified yoga instructor and teaches yoga for healing grief. She is the Affiliate Leader of the Phoenix/Scottsdale HPH group. Please visit the Helping Parents Heal website, www.helpingparentsheal.org

The honor of your journey
will be passed to those around you
in a synchronous way
for the intent of the one
will always affect the many

Words Spoken from the Light to
Claudia Watts Edge

In my early twenties, I lost a friend. *I hadn't spent time with him in several years, but the news hit me hard. This intelligent, talented and handsome young man had barely begun to explore all of his given talents before an unconscionable act was committed against him.*

He was senselessly murdered.

I could feel the pain of his sister, who could not fathom continuing to live in a world without her big brother beside her. They were close in age and in care of one another. I had brothers too, and I could relate.

But to witness the pain of a Mother's loss, there are just not the words to describe an unbridled grief that no parent should have to live through.

I cautiously approached her to offer my sincere condolences, and the words she whispered, still ring in my ears. She placed her hand on mine, and the other against the belly that carried my first child, and said,

"Just Love Them"

It was a seemingly simple statement offered from a mother to a soon to be mother, and it wasn't until I saw the poem he had written to her just months before his death, did I begin to understand the complexities of mothering, especially when the road they are traveling seems to be in direct opposition to what you have imagined for them.

I share his poem just as it was written all those years ago, saving it while discarding so many other collectables, because it is special, HE WAS SPECIAL. I share it to honor the Mothers here who told their own heart wrenching story of loss, but what they were able find in spite of it.

Answers

Worry not, oh Mother of mine, about the course of my deeds

They are, as it is often said about young men

Only attempts to fulfill tentative needs.

Look forward to the serene day when

Together we can regard these troubled days with a smile

And wonder why we let the differences rent us apart

Twas like trying to cut bread with a file

And trying to go through, instead of over each rampart

In the meanwhile, we must both have

The chance to reflect on one another's love

And sooth each other with it like a salve

But ready to part from it as one must with the dove

Although it may appear as if our relationship were at an end

In truth, as it were, it has just barely opened.

Prose: by Jeffrey Capel

October 1971 Dixie College St. George Utah

MY EASTER SURPRISE

When your world has been turned upside down

By Deb Kosmer

On October 25, 1989, my fourteen-year-old son was struck by a car and died. When the coroner came to our door to tell us, I felt like he'd stuck a knife in my heart. I wanted so badly for him to be at the wrong house, talking about the wrong kid, but he wasn't, and the nightmare began.

I don't remember much about those first few weeks and months, except how hard it seemed to breathe. I kept waiting for the nightmare to end, but it didn't. I didn't suddenly wake up and see my son sleeping in his bed, or have to tell him to turn his music down, those days ended with the ringing of a doorbell. Life as my family knew it was over.

Our house seemed so empty, and it just seemed to scream that Shawn was gone. There were reminders of him everywhere, all of the things he'd never use again. His brand-new bike hung in the garage, but I couldn't bring myself to part with it. His jackets were still in the hall closet. One of them was his prized Oshkosh West football jacket, and the other was his Oshkosh Northwestern jacket. The Northwestern was our local newspaper that he had delivered papers for, and the year before he died he was named 'Carrier of the Year' and given a large trophy engraved with those words, and his name and year. So many things left behind, all of which seemed to scream his name.

After our loved ones die their things take on new meaning and importance to us. The clothes they wore, the things their hands touched, these things that now keep us connected to them.

When we can now no longer touch or smell those we love, we touch and smell what they leave behind.

Grieving is like being in a no man's land. It is a place of loneliness, even in a crowd. We long for what we had in a sadness and anger that we can never have it again. It is a place where hope is non-existent or very hard to find, and difficult to live without. Just as their belongings can comfort us, I, like many grieving people longed for a sign that my son was okay. Days passed and turned into weeks and then months. Time takes on a confusing quality when grieving. It can seem like forever since our loved one died, and at the same time, it can feel like it was just yesterday.

Easter was coming and I was dreading it. Easter had always been a happy time, but my mood would not allow me to celebrate. I wanted to skip it. I couldn't get excited about church, egg hunts, Easter baskets or dinner, because I knew it would just make me miss Shawn even more. I desperately needed to have something good happen soon.

That something happened the day before Easter with a phone call. There was a message on our answering machine from a local handmade chocolate shop, saying that Shawn had won the drawing for the solid chocolate bunny. I knew there had to be some mistake. Was someone playing a cruel joke on us? Had they meant to call a different house with a boy named Shawn? My husband called the store and was told yes, they had called, and verified Shawn's name as the winner. I was confused, and as I headed to my car, I decided that someone in the family must have entered Shawn's name. When I got to the store and they brought out the bunny, I was amazed at the size of it. It was huge! I questioned everyone in my family, but each said they had not been to the store., and then I began to think that maybe one of his friends had done it, but then I stopped short. I realized it didn't matter how my son's name got in there and picked, all that mattered is that it happened. I felt a wave of peace wash over me as I thought it was Shawn's way of saying "I love you all, I'm ok. Please be okay for me, Happy Easter." I wrapped the message around my heart, and went to the refrigerator and got the eggs out.

Deb Kosmer,

debra.kosmer@icloud.com in memory of my son, Shawn J. Schmitz

FROM A MORTICIAN'S PERSPECTIVE

NEVER A BRIDESMAID, NEVER A BRIDE

By Chelsea Tolman

Death is a certainty. It comes in so many forms, ages, and types. Young un-expected deaths are a difficult reality and young expected deaths can be even more difficult. When a child knows they are so sick that they are going to die before they get to drive, go to prom, have a first kiss, or get married, the life they do experience carries more weight than for the rest of us. It becomes more about making the best of what you are given than to imagine what the future holds.

In this case it was a young girl, not yet thirteen. She had always been terminally ill. She knew that she would die young. She dreamed of doing the things that most girls her age do, like go to college or be a famous in some way. But what she wanted most was to be a bride, to wear the beautiful gown and have her hair curled and primped and be the center of attention for a day, her day.

In the weeks before her death she told her mother that she wanted to be buried as the bride she had dreamed of being. She wanted to pick out her gown and looked at pictures of hairstyles. The girl had gotten to a point where she couldn't leave the hospital anymore, so her mother had a manicurist come to her room and apply pink polish to her tiny, child hands.

She died a couple of weeks later.

I remember meeting her mother, and how she told me how much her daughter wanted to be dressed like a princess in pink layers and lots of sparkles. I watched the pain and sorrow in her mother's eyes as she described her child' s dream, knowing that she would never get to plan the Wedding, or gain a son-in-law or grandchild, only that she would buy the casket that would accent the gown and make the arrangements for her daughter's funeral. We planned out the details and the family went home.

The next day the mother walked into the mortuary bearing her daughter's gown. She carried it like a child, like it was her most prized possession, holding the hanger in one hand while the bulging plastic bag that protected the cherished dress draped over her other arm. Before she allowed me to take it from her hands, she told me the story of how she had spent time with her daughter shopping for the perfect dress, just weeks before she was permanently bed-ridden. She described to me how this young girl would try on dresses and giggle while turning around on the dress shop platform, admiring the flow of the fabrics around her legs and watching her reflection in the tall mirrors.

A mother's love is a powerful thing. For her to take her baby to wedding shops and endure the sidelong looks of the staff judging her for shopping for a wedding dress for one so young. Or have to answer, when questioned, that they were searching for a burial gown for this beautiful, young child. She watched and bore these moments that should have been for a planned wedding of a young woman and signify the beginning of a new life, not the end of one.

I was given the dress, which I carefully held in my arms in the same way mother had done. It was ceremonial, like passing a torch. After saying goodbye, I immediately went to the back rooms of the mortuary to uncover the dress wrapped in a plastic bag. It was a gown of pale cream with a hint of pink. The skirt had so many layers. Included was a slip that puffed with even more layers. The dress bore tiny bits of glitter nestled throughout the fabric that sparkled with every movement. The top was sleeveless and made of satin, the hint of pink gently peeking through when the light hit it just right. I hung it up on the back of a door and retied the bag to keep it protected.

The next day the beautician arrived at the mortuary. The girl was lying on a table in the center of one of our viewing rooms covered with a white sheet and on top of the sheet I had covered her with a burgundy blanket, neatly folded over at her shoulders.

Burgundy couches and dark wood end tables surrounded the room and stood against cream colored walls. I stayed in the room, watching as each curl was formed to become a lovely frame around the young girls' cherub face. Once finished, I thanked the beautician and walked her to the front door, then returned to the daughter, wheeled her into the back room once again and finished getting her ready.

Dressing this child was quite the experience. I wrestled with the layers that were designed to be placed on a bride who was standing up. Each layer had an agenda to move in its own direction and my attempt at forcing them to all behave in the manner I wanted, it would have been comical to watch I am sure. Layers snagged at my hair, flopped to the side, and stuck straight up in the air, absolutely refusing to lay down properly.

I finally had things arranged enough to finish the other details. With her hair neatly coifed and dress adorned I applied her makeup as her mother had instructed. Light powder, rosy cheeks, a hint of mascara and clear lip gloss was all that was needed.

Her casket was a light pink, shiny and perfectly accented to the bits of pink fabric in her dress. A coworker and I wrestled with the rows of uncooperative layers as we lifted the child in our arms and gently laid her down on the soft mattress resting her head on the shiny satin pillow. I spent some more time arranging the dress, attempting to make it all fit inside the boundaries of the casket. This was not to happen. The pouf that surrounded and rose above the child's thin legs, spilled off the sides of its intended vessel, refusing to be corralled. I stood back from the casket and looked at the child and casket she lay in. The dress was meant to be seen, so I left the casket fully open, revealing the entire gown with her tiny feet peeking out from the bottom encased in thin, pink tights.

I had scheduled for the family to come and visit the child before the day of the funeral. Once they had all arrived, I had them gather in front of the door to the viewing room where the girl awaited their arrival, the mother stood in front of everyone and was clearly anxious. I explained what they would be walking into. It was the same room that I had led the beautician into just the day before, only now the girl lay in her casket against the right-side wall of the room. I explained that the casket was open to show off the glittery folds of the prized wedding gown.

As I opened the door to the room and the family walked in, they were muted and subdued as they beheld the figure lying in a casket designed for those who had lived to grow old. I waited and listened as the silence turned to sniffles, then small cries and then the unforgettable wail of a grieving mother, a sound that hits your very heart and you will never forget.

Wordlessly, I left the room to give them time to mourn in private, and stood in the hallway just outside the door for whenever I was needed. A short time later the door cracked open and I was beckoned inside. The mother stood before me holding a pair of pale pink ballerina slippers. She explained that her daughter had taken ballet classes, so she thought the slippers were fitting and also, she wanted to be the one to place them on her daughter's feet but was afraid of doing it wrong or hurting her or breaking something. This is a common fear with people who are unfamiliar with the dead. She grabbed my hand and walked me to the foot of the casket, reluctantly letting my hand go as I talked her through what to do. Then we placed a halo of little white embroidered flowers with yellow centers around the crown of the girl 's head, and she truly looked like an angel. The moment was precious, and I watched her mother's heart break as she prepared to bury her child bride.

Chelsea Tolman, Salt Lake City, Utah Funeral Director, Interventionist and Psychiatric Technician.

Funeral service found its way into her life after watching coworkers struggle with death and seeing first-hand how much impact a funeral director can have on the grieving. She attended college at Gupton-Jones College of Mortuary Science in Decatur, GA. That was a time and place where women in the funeral industry were virtually unheard of. She has a great passion for teaching others kindness and patience when serving grieving families.

She has been interviewed on radio shows, podcasts, blogs, publications and TV, all links can be found on her website www.ChelseaTolman.com. In November 2018 she published her first book "Speaking of the Dead" which quickly gained interest with the public as well as the funeral community. She has since retired from funeral service and is now working in the mental health field in the Salt Lake City area.

Dear reader,

Yes, this story broke my heart too, and I write now with a lump in my throat. Though this story does not include the spiritual transformative aha's as the rest of these stories do, I felt strongly that it had something important to teach. As Chelsea stated at the beginning of her story, death is a certainty, and it comes in many forms, ages, and types. Chelsea would know, as she is a seasoned funeral director, and has handled the underpinnings of death up close and personal for over 20 years. I met her at the bedside of my mother after her unrelenting battle to remain on this Earth was lost.

This beautiful woman of 85 years left this world in a state not recognizable to her own self, her body whittled down to skin over bones, her beautiful hair had not been able to be washed or styled for months. Breathing tubes had left her mouth frozen open, and the stillness of her heart had erased the living flush of pale pink, her skin now a dingy yellow-grey. I had never met Chelsea before this day, but I trusted her immediately with the vessel of my beloved Mother, my instincts telling me to give what had been my commission and command during this long hospital stay over to her now, and that she would do what needed to be done in as gentle and respectable a way as my mother deserved.

There is much behind the scenes of a tattered body leaving the hospital and appearing days later in the funeral home as a closer resemblance to your loved one. It is important work done for those left behind, and no amount of knowing and or believing that they are in a 'better place' can take away the sting of the loss of the physical presence and the ability to go to the movies or share a meal together.

This is an important time for the living who are left in a wake of goodbyes and finality, trying to get used to the new normal of their absence. I applaud the mother in Chelsea's story for looking beyond what others might think of the style of clothing chosen to be buried in, or the personal style of what to do with the remains for that matter.

My own birthday is the last day of May in the days when it directly followed Memorial Day, or Decoration Day, as my family called it. Our family had a large burial plot in the small town cemetery. It was purchased by my mother and her sisters, who intended to stay close, even in death.

In my youth, my birthday parties were held at this cemetery, my cousins and I running between the stones bearing names we knew. I grew up feeling comfortable there, with balloons, water fights and birthday cake, but also grew comfortable with the idea of a coffin and burial. Many of my friends feel it barbaric to put the body into the ground, exposed to nature's eventual retrieval, and dust to dust, but we grow accustomed to tradition, and this is mine.

Cremation for many is the only way, a chance to hold the ashes, whether displayed in a beautiful urn, or given back to nature by their own hand, tossed into the air in favorite spot of the deceased. I have learned of the many countries that use a funeral pyre in the open air, and found that there are very few places in the United States where this cost effective and frankly beautiful send-off is allowed. See Crestone Colorado open air cremation. crestoneeagle.com

I used to tell my mother, the funeral is more for the living than the dead, and she would laugh and say, "OK, then I will just leave it up to you," but it is much harder than it sounds to plan that memorial, trying to find the words that might make a difference and soften the circle of grief for those who remain.

This book of stories of miraculous events is meant to find openings in the minds and hearts of those fearful of this inevitable process, and what comes after. 'They are not gone, but only in the next room,' and the ceremony and celebration of your transition from a caterpillar to a butterfly should be anything you want it to be, and wearing anything you want to wear.

Claudia Watts Edge

Chapter Ten

MISCARRIAGE

"NO HEARTBEAT, NO MOVEMENT AND IT'S A BREACH."

By Frank D'Silva

Divya was born in a small city in southern India. She was an only child and had a good childhood. Her father was easy going while her mother was a strict housewife. Even though her parents bought her most things, she always craved for love and affection.

After completing her studies in college, she met her husband. It was love at first sight. She went against her parent's wishes and got married. It was the love and happiness that she yearned for. Dining out, going to movies, shopping, and other things she would be able to do all on her own.

But the love slowly started fading. Even though her husband loved her, he was a different person when he drank alcohol, and he would abuse her physically as well as emotionally. After two years of marriage she finally fell pregnant. She felt a lot of joy, happiness, and excitement as she thought of her future child. But her husband was not as excited with the news and he still kept drinking and abusing her. So in her last few months of pregnancy she decided to stay with her parents to keep away from her husband's abuse.

When the seventh month was up, Divya was very happy and excited as she went to a local hospital for a routine medical check-up. She met the doctor who spent a lot of time examining her. She was told that they needed to get a scan of the baby. Her motherly instincts kicked in and Divya started getting a bit nervous and started praying. She sat there waiting for the results with her fingers crossed.

The Loss

As Divya sat waiting in the hospital, the doctor finally came in with the report. With shaking hands she read it in disbelief, it said "No heartbeat, no movement and it's a breach." The doctor softly said that she had lost her baby.

Divya's world collapsed. She felt all life force sucked out of her. She cried her lungs out and people in the hospital tried to console her. But nothing could stop her. She went crying to other doctors asking if they could find her baby's heartbeat and to tell her that her baby was okay, but no one could help her.

She was admitted to the hospital for surgery to remove the fetus. The surgery was done late at night and when Divya saw her baby she cried. "He was blue and lifeless. I could not hold him and kiss him goodbye." She was angry with God, angry with her husband, and blamed herself for the loss.

The Recovery

Losing one's baby is one of the most painful experiences a mother can go through. The pain cannot be easily forgotten and recovery and healing is a slow process. Divya tried for another child, going through various tests and IVF treatment. She was exhausted answering queries from family and friends as she still could not conceive. She started losing her self-confidence and the urge to live. She was gaining weight and getting depressed.

Finally she came across a doctor who started her on yoga and physical exercise. She also started pursuing her childhood hobbies like painting and jewelry making. Yoga boosted her self-confidence and she also started listening to music.

Visit to the Spirit World

Many years have passed since Divya lost her baby. Early in January 2020, she had to have her uterus removed and was going through major issues with her marriage and health. One of her friends told her to contact a man named Frank who helped people who had lost their loved ones. Divya was not keen on this idea. She began avoiding her friend's calls because he kept suggesting this whenever he talked to her. Finally, just to keep her friend happy she decided to contact Frank.

Frank D'Silva, based in Perth, Australia had trained under the world-famous American Doctor, Brian Weiss, a Past Life Regressionist and author of many books, including 'Many Lives Many Masters.'

During the initial phone conversation, he gave Divya a brief explanation of the Soul. "We are Spiritual Beings created a long time ago by God, with a Soul and Free Will. As part of our learning and development we come to this planet in a human form. After we pass away we shed our human body and our Spirit goes back home to the Spirit World." During between Lives sessions, one can enter the Spirit World through deep meditation and connect with loved ones who have passed into the afterlife. Divya felt very calm and assured by Frank's explanation. Slowly she opened up and told her story about the loss of her child, her health issues, and her anxiety attacks. She felt she needed to heal and asked for an appointment.

On the day of the session Divya was a bit nervous. Frank calmed her and assured her that she would be fine and started her with simple breathing exercises followed by relaxation and visualization techniques. Divya could not relax and Frank then asked her to let go of the grief and blame she was carrying. As Frank guided her deeper into relaxation, she suddenly felt very light and calm. She felt she was floating in the Spirit World. She felt a white light surrounding her with love and her guide's hand blessing her. Then Frank asked, "Divya do you want to meet your baby?" Her answer was a resounding "Yes."

Suddenly Divya felt a beautiful baby in her arms. She could sense, feel, and smell her baby for the first time. She cried and cried. She could see the smile and happiness on her baby's face. She felt very happy and joyful and did not want it to end. She asked her baby "Why did you leave me?" The baby answered, "I was afraid."

That day was the turning point of Divya's life as she was able to leave her anxiety and sadness behind. With a heart full of love, hope, and a new sense of purpose, Divya is now slowly putting her past behind and looking forward to a life with renewed purpose. She has also decided to reach out to other grieving mothers as part of her healing.

Frank D'Silva, Perth, Australia
Certified Hypnotherapist trained under Dr Brian Weiss

I wanted to note here that many people may not have heard of this form of therapy, but it is gaining a lot of attention as many spiritual workers are entering this field of relaxed regression therapy.

For more information on Guided Past Life Regression, and Life-Between-Lives Hypnotherapy Regression, there are many local affiliates trained in the Brian Weiss and Dr Michael Newton techniques.

A LESSON OF TRUE LOVE AND TRUE LOSS

By Jennifer Ann

I had a miscarriage at approximately 8 weeks gestation in 2018. When I was pregnant, I was blessed enough to hear the baby's heartbeat at about 6-7 weeks, but the baby died shortly after. I had felt her energy, and it was amazing and I will always hold onto this beautiful knowledge of her.

After my miscarriage, I went inward and began meditating a lot. The soul of my daughter came through when she was about 5 years old, and she helped me to understand that she is with my grandmother until I cross over.

Spirit did give me a choice, that I could just wait until then to meet my baby, or I could get pregnant again and bring her soul through. This was a very hard decision, considering I'm a pediatric cancer survivor, and getting pregnant in the first place was a miracle. I unfortunately had to choose to wait, because my body just could not handle another pregnancy. I am very lucky to have a 5-year-old biological child, but my pregnancy with him was really rough, and I am so grateful he is here and I get to be his mommy.

Spirit told me that it was ok and not to judge myself. I will be with my baby again, and she does come through from time to time when I need her most. My baby angel reminds me that she taught me what true loss feels like, so now I know true love from son who I have on earth, and true loss from my angel baby on the other side. I am very grateful for both lessons...even if the latter was so very painful to learn.

Some souls come back, though some souls have already done what they were meant to before ever being born. This is what I learned from my experiences.

Jennifer Ann

Chapter Eleven

HEAVENLY CONTACT

HELLO FROM THE OTHER SIDE

A reminder not to believe in

weakness or fear

but to restore belief in YOURSELF

by accepting

that YOU are

A Teacher of Light in the Making

Claudia Watts Edge

THE NIGHT HOURS

Dreams are brought to life as images

That play on the innermost side of the eyelid

Grief, Regrets, Happiness, Forgiveness, Fear, Anxiety, Social Connections,

Power Struggles, Sexual Tension, Jealousy, Perceived Inadequacy, Pride,

Accomplishments, Loss, Loneliness, Trust Issues and Joy,

are examples of the lessons we work through

as we role play in the night school we call Dreams.

Claudia Watts Edge

MY GRANDMOTHER RANG US THE DAY OF HER FUNERAL

By Penny Freeman

O ur family, distracted by the day's events did not move when the phone rang. It was one of the grandchildren who answered the call, bounding into our circle of conversation to relay a message... A lady named Peggy just rang to tell us "she is well, and she loves us all." We nearly dropped as Peggy, although unknown to the child, was our grandmothers name, and to whom we had just said our final goodbyes.

Penny Freeman, Dungog, New South Wales Australia

There are signs and symbols our loved ones use to get our attention. If we pay attention we will learn and recognize when they are sending messages. This is also true when we send out our thoughts to them. We are all spiritual beings with unlimited potential, and we can sense and connect with the 'other realm' because we are and will always be connected to each other.

A TWINKLING BIRTHDAY VISIT

By Kathleen Sterling

My birthday is on New Year's Day and my mother and I made plans to celebrate it together. But sadly, everything changed on December 16 when she passed away after a long battle with cancer. I am blessed to have a close circle of friends, and of the six of us, two had also suffered a loss in that same month.

We decided to lift ourselves up and celebrate my birthday in a fun girls' night with lots of love and support surrounding our special circle.

While laughing and enjoying each other's company, I noticed something out of the corner of my eye. The battery-operated Christmas candles began to twinkle, and I walked across the room for a closer look. I couldn't believe my eyes! The bulb portion wasn't even screwed into the light socket so how could it be "twinkling?"

Then, while all of us watched, the bulb turned fully on, and stayed on.

I just knew it was my Mom, and I started talking to the light, thanking her for coming to my birthday party, all while my friends stared in amazement.

After many moments, I turned my attention back toward my friends and they all gasped and told me that when I turned around, the light had gone out, so I sat back down, keeping my eye on the light that immediately went back to twinkling. This was so much her fun-loving personality, and I said aloud "Mom always did like a good party" and we all giggled together and thanked her for coming.

A week had passed when my friend got her holiday pictures back, and she could hardly contain herself. At the top of a photo was an image of my mother's spirit hovering over my friend's daughter. She was determined that I know that she was with us, and that she had kept our date of celebrating my birthday together.

I keep this picture next to her alter, and when I shared this beautiful experience with my sister, she asked how come mom didn't come to her, and I replied, "I asked."

Kathleen Sterling, Des Moines WA

These beautiful stories of our departed loved ones have been the mortar in my personal foundation of understanding that communication beyond the veil is possible. Our loved ones are forever connected to us, and they are aware of our lives and upcoming events. I just love the simplicity of Kathleen's answer because it rings of more than simple belief and more like an expected result. "I asked" sums up it up perfectly.

Chapter Twelve

DREAM COMMUNICATION

MORE THAN A DREAM

By Sharlan Oskins

I t's been a long hard year, though for me it is not because of the state of the world or even the COVID pandemic. I lost somebody. She was my best friend, and I miss her.

We did everything together, making a point to create memories of happy silly times. We could find the fun in any given situation, even as we stayed up all night for the Black Friday after Thanksgiving sales. We would take videos of ourselves both singing and dancing in the aisles during long checkout lines, and we created characters in funny get-ups while trying on hats and glasses from the displays near the checkout counters. We knew how to keep ourselves and the surrounding audience of serious bargain shoppers entertained. Each and every video showed that she was always in the middle of the fun.

It is worth noting that she had more energy than all of the rest of us pooled together, a pint-sized force of nature, and I am proud to say that this friend of mine was also my mother. I watched this woman in both admiration and amazement every day of my life.

I took notice when her memory began to slip, accepting it as a result of her age and her approaching eighties, but when her trademark dish of creamy potato salad showed up as a bowl full of perfectly seasoned, RAW POTATOES, everyone else was forced to acknowledged it too.

Grammie would soon be diagnosed with a heartless disease called Dementia, a silent thief of the mind. Remembering to eat, bathe, and turn off the stove were all in question, and I was helpless to stop its claim on her independence. The freedom to drive to her full-time job would be replaced by a full-time living facility.

Her life was being stolen out from under her, and the precious memories we created together would soon be mine alone.

I marveled at her grace in her last year as she refused to give up her zest for life. She remained front and center at family gatherings, making the rounds with sodas and trays of cookies, and a sincere question of "what can I get for you?" She would smile at the faces in front of her and say, "I may not remember who you are, but I know that I love you!" and then give a warm, loving hug. It fills me with pride that although her mind had been altered, her heart was never touched. It held love for everyone around her, a legacy that would remain, even after she was gone.

It had been weeks since her passing, and my grief was still raw as I dealt with the aftermath and legal paperwork that is needed to close down a life. It was while reading the physician's report that I learned that her Earthly battle had been a much harder fight than any of us knew. I stared in disbelief at the revelation that she had lived for over seven years knowing that while her mind was slowly fading, her lungs were waging a battle with cancer.

Gramie had made a hard-fast decision not to submit herself to the same body ravaging treatments she had watched the love of her life go through years before. A firm stance of rejecting attention also meant that none of us were to even know about it. There would be no discussion or family meetings of how to proceed with probabilities of extending her life, she was unwavering in this decision. There was no possibility for voicing any challenges, and she carried this determination to the very end.

It had been two weeks since we had parked ourselves beside her bed and watched the life clock of this amazing woman wind down to its final hours. What a blessing it was to have the entire family gathered around her as we shared stories, tears, and chuckles. We were still making memories, and we felt her with us even though we may not have been able to hear her laughter.

In the end, she exercised her valued independence one last time. She waited for me and my brothers to finally close our eyes and drift into sleep before taking her leave with the same dignity and grace she held in her life. She was an independent woman who would choose her own time, and her own way.

The knowledge of her having cancer became a question that stayed in the forefront of my mind, and I just couldn't let it go, "why she would choose to go through it all alone," and I expressed my frustration until exhaustion finally took me over, forcing me to lay down while I cried. As sleep began to claim me, I asked my question once again, just in case she was listening.

I woke to the sound of the doorbell. The fact that it was the middle of the night didn't seem unusual as I got out of bed to answer it. Although it was winter, I did not feel cold, and I did not stop to reach for my robe or slippers but rather walked down the darkened hallway toward the front of the house.

The air around me seemed to have a peaceful calm as I opened the door to a flood of white light. Its golden brilliance seemed to turn the night into day, illuminating and surrounding a familiar form that stood on my front porch. I recognized her immediately, it was my mother.

I was so happy to see her, she was beaming the same smile I remembered before illness began to take its toll. She looked free of worry and pain, and her hair and make-up looked perfect. I gave a quick happy laugh as I fumbled to get the screen door opened saying "Mom, what are you doing here?" and as I ran in her direction, her arms opened wide inviting me to climb inside of them.

The warmth of our embrace carried a lifetime of love and friendship within it, and I didn't want to let her go. Eventually I asked my question, "Oh My God Mom, did you know you had cancer?" I suspected that I already knew the answer, but really needed to hear it from her. "Yes, I did know." "Why didn't you tell us?" She looked directly into my eyes and said, "I didn't want you guys to worry" and without any other words needed, I knew instantly that it was not her intention to add any burden onto me or the rest of the family to carry and that she had come back to make it right and to take away my questioning.

I have lived my life saying I don't dream, or if I do dream I don't remember, but this was different. I saw my mother standing so naturally on my doorstep, the light all around her was so brilliant it seemed to turn night into the middle of the day, and I can barely speak without crying for the feelings of a lifetime of love that we were able to share in that last hug... THAT WAS REAL.

To this day I can still close my eyes, and see her standing there smiling at me, and within that smile I can feel her telling me that everything is going to be alright.

I have kept this event close to my heart because I consider it sacred, and I am only sharing it now in the hopes it will give comfort to someone who is also suffering a hard loss.

There is much I do not understand of these matters, but there are some things I know for sure; my mother came to me in a dream to let me know that she is happy and can still hear me, and that the friendship and love we have for each other will never die.

Sharlan Oskins, West Jordan, Utah

BLESS YOU

By Mila Andelman

Shortly after my husband passed away, I began to journal my dreams. I just had to capture the dreams on paper as there were so many beautiful expressions of connection to him, and although I am not a writer, I will try to describe one of them here.

The loss of my husband was very hard on me. It felt as if I was barely coming to grips with the rest of my life when my husband's best friend also passed away 10 months later, almost to the day. Everything in my life was changing and I desperately needed something to hang onto, and then this dream came to me at the two-week mark of our friend's transition.

We are at a big party, my husband Lev, myself, and our friend Valera. We were all dressed up, the guys looking so young and happy. We were all smiles, so happy to be together. A woman with beautiful auburn hair caught our attention as she walked across the stage at the other end of the room. She was looking toward me and addressing the song to me! It was magical, the melody so beautiful and she repeated these words of the song: "Bless you, bless you," as she was looking directly into my eyes!

I knew I was experiencing the joy of the life after life; I know it exists! Believe me! I was so very happy, and as the dream began to end, I realized that I was now walking home on a familiar street in my old country of Ukraine.

My dream/experience was ending, but I was able to stop and take one last good look around me as I walked away. It was all so beautiful, the grand trees and flowers of unimaginable colors!

When I woke I felt so much peace, as if I had been given a gift to see what my husband and his friend were able to see, and also, what they were feeling. They were so very happy, and I knew that they wanted me to live on, to notice all things, to enjoy my life, and like the words of the song said, "bless you." I knew that I was watched over and loved, and that someday I would join them in a similar celebration.

Mila Andelman,
Ukraine,Vancouver BC Canada

Life

Is an exercise of faith...

It is an agreement to give away each breath

In exchange for the next

Claudia Watts Edge

Chapter Thirteen

SUICIDE INTROSPECTION

SUICIDE INTROPECTION

By Enos Anderson

From a human perspective suicide is seen as negative, selfish, cowardly, or even heroic. How it is perceived depends on many variables, such as: did you love the person, was the person ailing, was the person suffering from depression, was it an act of cowardice to escape punishment, or was it a sacrifice to save another?

But what is suicide in reality? It is a choice made by a soul to exit a life before its pre-planned exit. From a soul perspective it is neither good nor bad; it is an event. Why do souls sometimes opt for an early exit? I think sometimes when we plan a life on Earth we can be overly brave and take on more than we can handle in one lifetime, or we could get bored with a life or maybe the vessel has become useless because of physical incapacity. To the soul making that decision the reasons are enough, it is not for us to judge. Very often loved ones left behind react with disbelief, anger, and depression—and on rare occasions, understanding.

When a soul opts for an early exit it does affect others who were participating in that soul's plan, and scripts have to be rewritten to accommodate the early exit of a player. It also affects that soul in that experiences hoped for will be delayed. On the bright side it might provide an opportunity for connected souls to learn some valuable lessons, such as unconditional love and how to deal with heart-wrenching loss through acceptance.

Is a soul punished for choosing suicide when it returns home? No, there is no judgement at home, no punishment, just love and understanding. This soul will accept that its choice has delayed its progress and will plan a new reincarnation to catch up to where it left off. If the soul was severely affected it might require a period of adjustment to get its energy cleansed and recharged.

Suicide then is neither evil nor good, it is a choice made by a soul and its consequence is only a delay in moving up the ladder of enlightenment. It could also provide learning opportunities for associated souls.

Enos Anderson JP, Ct, Hyp., PLR

Trinidad and Tobago. Excerpt from his book: WE HAVE LIVED BEFORE is used by permission

A GIFT FROM THE OTHER SIDE

After my Friend's Suicide

By Fiona Sutton

I had been a close friend of Jon for many years. He had a giving and tender heart, but I watched him over-give in his relationships, seemingly setting himself up for eventual rejection and a broken heart. From early on in our acquaintance, told me he was not going to make it to thirty years, and then he took his own life at the age of 29. He had killed himself because the woman he proposed to had turned him down. He couldn't cope with the rejection, so sat in the garage with the car running. While I struggled with the loss, I was angry at him too. How unfair of him to place such heavy burdens of guilt on all of us he had left behind.

Was there something anyone of us could have done?

He seemed to be determined to fulfill the earlier promise he had made in anger over a previous break-up. He felt he had been done wrong and wanted to end the pain. I had spent a lot of time trying to convince him otherwise. It gets tiring to keep someone alive that seems so set on ending it. Our talks were immediate fixes, but apparently his problems were more than I, or any of his other friends or family, could handle. Now we were living in the wake of his decision with grief, loss, frustration, and anger. I knew that I also had a decision to make and so I continued to fully live my own life, though my thoughts would often come around to him. I questioned, was he happy now, or was he stuck in some kind of dark regret about his decision?

As I became more spiritually aware, I developed more understanding and compassion. I recognized that in a lot of respects he just didn't seem to fit into this world. He was so kind and big-hearted, he felt things so deeply, craving the kind of love that he just couldn't seem to obtain. I eventually made my peace with him, hoping that he had found what had so eluded him on this earthly plane.

One evening, after a bad day at work, I felt unusually low and disheartened. As I meditated, I asked, if during the night I could be comforted by something from the higher realms. Since entering this spiritual phase of life, unicorns and rainbows have become very significant to me, for too many reasons to go into here. I decided that I would particularly like to be sent a unicorn, and I went to sleep thinking the words, "Please send me a unicorn."

Well, the long and short of it is that I received something better. The dream was far more vivid than is usual for me, and on waking at 3:00am in the morning, I could remember every detail. Jon appeared in the dream, looking happy and radiant. I was so delighted to see him. Tellingly, there was a woman with him. This comforted me, because I now felt that he had found his soul mate. The love that emanated from him can only be described as heavenly love. It was so comforting and joyful, much more intense than the love you feel on Earth, and I was reflecting the same love back to him.

In the dream, I was having electrical problems, and Jon explained that he had appeared to help me out. "Whenever you need help," he stated, "I will always be here for you." Electrics sorted, he left. Later in the dream, I was clearing a barn out in the stables where we had met and enjoyed spending time together. I was hating the job of brushing out cobwebs and spiders, and I was wishing I had help. Jon appeared again, repeating the same message as before. He sorted it for me, and left.

Then I awoke with a start. I couldn't doubt the reality of the dream. Not only had it been incredibly vivid, but on awakening, I still felt the joy and love that I had experienced in the dream. Also, my ears were roaring (something that happens when I am having spiritual experiences) to the extent that my eyes were actually watering.

But the story doesn't end there. About a week later, on visiting my parents, my mum informed me that she had been having a sort out, and had found some things I had been gifted over the years. Everything she produced, I could remember being given, except for one thing; a sculpture of a mother and baby unicorn, with a rainbow-colored crystal ball at their feet. I stared at it in disbelief. My two favorite things at the moment; a unicorn and rainbow. But however thoroughly I searched my memory, I could not remember ever having laid eyes on it before, let alone knowing who had gifted it to me. It was like I was seeing it for the first time. I looked at mum blankly, but she just looked bemused. "Can't you remember? It was from your friend Jon." She assured me that it was definitely him, and that she remembered it clearly.

Some people may say it is just a coincidence, but for me, it goes way beyond that. I had left home twenty years ago, so why was this being handed to me now? Why no knowledge of it, yet my mum could remember? More significantly, my interest in unicorns and rainbows had only materialized in the last year, not twenty or thirty years ago, when it was gifted to me. And the night that Jon appeared, I had asked for a unicorn to be sent to me.

It may seem far-fetched, but this whole sequence of events feels very special. I believe not only that Jon appeared in my dream to comfort and reassure me, but also that I received a gift from beyond the grave. He may have bought it years earlier, but circumstances have worked in such a way that it is like he gifted it to me now, not then. It now has pride of place on the cabinet next to my bed.

It is hard to express how much joy and comfort this dream visitation has brought me, gifting me with the knowledge that our loved ones can still help and support us from the other side. More importantly, I have proof that Jon has found the peace and happiness he so deserves. This is a true blessing indeed!

Fiona Sutton,

West Midlands England, Author of 'SEEKER OF THE LIGHT' and soon to be published 'A HORSE'S VOICE' with all book proceeds going to animal charities.

MY MIRACLE ON 34TH STREET

By Caroline Chang

My son Kyle's last words to me in this physical realm were "Ma, I don't want you to wait alone." He was being wheeled into the operating room for open heart surgery and he did not want me in the surgical waiting room by myself. He had good reason to be concerned about me, but that is the last thing he should be worrying about as he was being wheeled into open heart surgery. He asked me to call my brother so I would not be alone, and I told him I would, knowing full well that I could not. Because at that moment my brother was on a plane to Florida to see his daughter's final track meet. Kyle was not aware of this and I did not want to tell him, as the last thing I wanted was for Kyle to worry about me. I knew he was frightened about having the surgery even though he did not want me to know how frightened he really was.

Kyle had good reason to be concerned about me waiting alone. It was just two and half years earlier when doctors had told me they did not think Kyle was going to live; and at that moment I was determined not to go home without my son. I never told him exactly what had happened during that time in the hospital in December 2011, and the steps I took to make that happen. Somehow, he instinctively knew, it was a heart and soul knowing just between us.

Our shared spiritual pilgrimage began on Wednesday, November 23, 2011. It was the night before Thanksgiving, which also happened to be the night before Kyle's 27th birthday. Thanksgiving has always been my favorite holiday, a day to be together with family and friends, eat good food and give THANKS! I wish it would get just as much attention as Christmas; instead, there is very little emphasis placed on a holiday that is not wrapped up in religious dogma and consumer shopping.

I love everything about Thanksgiving Day! I'll never forget when I was very little, one of my fondest memories from my childhood was hanging around the kitchen watching my Dad cook Thanksgiving dinner. The air would fill with the wonderful aroma of green peppers, onions, celery and Parks sausage sautéing on the stove for my Dad's famous sausage stuffing (It was famous to me). Every year since my very first year as a young bride of just 17, I would do my best to make my Dad's stuffing just the way he did for Thanksgiving. However, this particular Thanksgiving dinner in November 2011, I was planning to make a completely "Heart Healthy" dinner without my Dad's sausage stuffing, because Kyle had been diagnosed with Congestive Heart Failure (CHF) just a few months earlier.

He had just recently come home from the hospital, his third stay, thus far that year. I wanted to do whatever I could possibly do to help Kyle get healthy holistically and naturally. I was planning a low-carb, heart healthy Thanksgiving and Birthday dinner for just the two of us.

I had invited other family members to join us, however no one else was coming. It was going to be just us two, for Thanksgiving/Birthday dinner that year.

That Wednesday night Kyle had made plans to go out and celebrate his birthday with his best friend Chris, who was the DJ at a local pub. Chris was coming to pick Kyle up, but Kyle would never tell me these things beforehand; I would always find out the moment he was halfway out the door. I happened to be in the middle of teaching a piano lesson when Kyle called out to me, he was having trouble breathing. I immediately dialed 911 for an ambulance, and the paramedics quickly arrived, checking his vital signs. He seemed to be feeling better, but they felt it would be best to take him to the hospital, more for observation than anything else. Kyle felt well enough to walk down the stairs and to the ambulance without assistance, saying "Oh, I won't be able to celebrate my birthday with Chris now!" That was the first I was learning he had plans to go out that night.

The next morning I called the hospital and spoke with Kyle, and asked him if he still wanted me to make the "Heart Healthy" Thanksgiving/ Birthday dinner and bring it to him in his hospital room; I wanted to be sure he felt up to eating before I started cooking. He gave me an ecstatic "Yes!" and so I started to cook, planning to get to the hospital with his dinner by 3:00 pm. I really do not understand what happened between the time I spoke with him about 9:00 am that morning and 1:00 pm, when doctors called me to let me know Kyle was on life support and I needed to get there right away. They didn't want me to drive myself, but what was I to do? It was Thanksgiving Day and I had no one to call, and so I drove myself to the hospital.

They had moved him to ICU, and this was my first time ever seeing Kyle on life support with a ventilator tube in his throat to breathe; at that moment my heart sank, I was so afraid of losing my "baby boy." He had severe pneumonia, his lungs were filled with fluids and his heart was extremely weak. I did not leave his side for the next 36 hours. The next evening things were looking a little better. His vital signs seemed to be improving, and a nurse suggested I take the opportunity to run home and take a shower. He seemed to be resting and out of danger at that moment, and it sounded like a good idea. I thought, I'll just run home and freshen up with a quick shower and clean clothes; I would be coming right back. Again, I do not know what happened but as I was home in the shower the phone rang; it was the hospital calling to tell me they were preparing to Medevac Kyle to the University Hospital of Pennsylvania (HUP) and for me to get back to the hospital quickly. I was still in the shower when I picked up the phone and fell to my knees with the water still running, truly in a state of shock, finding it hard to breathe.

When I left my house to go back to the hospital, I clearly remember thinking that I would never return home again, ever. I felt in my heart there was a good chance I would not be bringing my son home, and I would not go back there without him. When I got to his ICU room, they were preparing him for the Medevac helicopter which was on the roof of the hospital. They would not allow me to ride in the helicopter and I was in no condition to drive the long two-hour drive to Philadelphia at night. I don't see as well as I used to at night anymore, and Kyle would always tease me about my driving at night. He would say, "Ma, you drive kinda fast during the day, but at night it's like watching paint dry."

My friend's husband Larry offered to drive me the long way to Philadelphia, which was a miracle and a blessing I will never forget! While Larry drove, he kept speaking encouraging words to me the entire ride. I truly appreciated his support and encouragement; it was so needed. I knew he was just trying to keep me from thinking the worst. I remembered kissing Kyle on his forehead just before they took him up to the roof, thinking it might be the last time I would ever kiss my son. And as I watched the helicopter pull away, the only thought going through my head was, "I am not going home without my son." If Kyle wasn't coming home neither was I.

When I arrived at the hospital, my brother and his wife were already there; they live closer to Philadelphia, in Central NJ. I'll never forget how relieved I was when I spoke with the doctors there in the Cardiac ICU, they were very encouraging and they didn't make it seem like Kyle was in any danger, they had it all under control. I felt so relieved and much better with him being there rather than at Pocono Medical. HUP is one of the Top 10 hospitals in the country for cardiac care, open heart surgery and heart transplants. At that point I just knew Kyle would be in good hands, and all would be OK. I thought.

Kyle arrived at HUP in Philadelphia the night of November 25, 2011 on life support, and was admitted to the Cardiac ICU; he was still on life support for the next few weeks, and even though the doctor's initial reports when he arrived were very promising, there were a lot of ups and downs with Kyle's condition. I am glad there was a pullout chair that could double as a bed because I was determined to stay with him in the ICU.

On December 7, 2011, the doctors asked me to meet with them in a small waiting room, outside of Kyle's room. They asked me if they could take Kyle off life support because they didn't think he was going to make it, feeling his heart was not strong enough to overcome the pneumonia. I was in disbelief! I told them "NO!" I said, "Give Kyle my heart, my heart is strong enough!" Of course, they told me they could not do that; and even if they were able to do that, they said my heart would be too small, as Kyle was twice my size.

I knew at that point it was time for me to make my exit! The words I had repeated over and over again in my head on that long ride to Philadelphia, that I would not go back home without my son, needed to happen! Spiritually I know there is no death and that the soul lives on. I also know that there is truly no escape from life; that we choose to come here for a purpose and that our soul's purpose will have to be played out here or in another lifetime. However, I could not see myself living on without him; this was something I was determined not to live through. After the doctors had spoken to me, I do not remember if I went back into Kyle's ICU room right away. I was in a daze, and I was determined to leave this screen in the movie of my own creation.

There was no one I could call, no one I could talk to who I thought might have the slightest understanding of what I was going through or who could really be there for me at that moment. I just knew that I did not want to exist here in this physical realm anymore without my son, and I was trying to figure out how to get what I needed to do the trick; and put an end to this scene.

There was a pharmacy in the hospital lobby, I did not have a prescription and all I could find was over the counter sleeping pills and Tylenol. Well, I figured if I take the whole bottle of sleeping pills that would do it. I went to the 10th floor of the hospital where I knew there was a small private waiting room. I had been living in the hospital so long I was really getting to know my way around. Kyle's room was on the 8th floor on the Cardiac ICU wing, and I had noticed this room a few days earlier. It was a room that I never saw anyone in, it was out of the way and quiet and even had a homey feel to it. I made myself comfortable on the sofa, and got out a piece of paper and pen from the laptop bag I had kept with me the entire time I was living in the hospital. It came in very handy because I could sometimes get some work done in Kyle's ICU room during the times his vitals were looking good and he was on the up-swing.

I wrote my suicide note stating, "I am not going to bury my son, my son is going to bury me!" There was much more in the note, however that statement is what stands out in my mind. I took almost all the sleeping pills; it was hard to swallow because I was trying to swallow all of them at once. I also took some of the Tylenol, but not too many of them, I didn't think they were really needed, and I didn't want to make myself so sick that I would throw-up all of the pills, that would have done me no good. I laid down on the sofa, closed my eyes, and waited to drift off to sleep and never wake up. Well at least not wake up here.

I do remember my heart beating really fast and pounding through my chest, and that was the last thing I remembered until hearing the doctor who was trying to wake me up in the ER. He was shaking me and asking me "How many of these pills did you take?" while holding up one of the sleeping pills in front of my face. Even though I was only semi-conscious, I clearly remembered thinking, "Is he seriously asking me how many pills I took?" I replied fully aware of what I was saying when I answered him, "One!" I felt a silly question deserved a silly answer; and then I was out again, completely unconscious after delivering my "comical" response.

I honestly do not know what happened to me physically after taking an overdose of over the counter sleeping pills; I have never inquired about my medical records from that incident. All I knew was I was not supposed to still be here in this earthly realm. I was unconscious for two and half days, before I opened my eyes again. I was in the ICU and Kyle's young intern doctor, Dr. Ty, was standing at the foot of my bed saying, "Kyle needs you!" I remember those words so clearly, realizing that Kyle was still hanging on. I was still semi-unconscious but could hear my brother, his wife Michelle, and my cousin Lisa in the room with me.

For the next day or so I was in and out of consciousness and I vaguely remember a team of interns with their mentoring doctor asking me a host of questions. I do not remember the questions, but I do remember saying "I don't want to be here!" There was a young nurse's aide that whispered to me, "Don't keep saying you don't want to be here; because they will commit you." I heeded her warning and didn't say that again.

When my vital signs were well enough to move me out of the ICU to a regular room the hospital had me on 24-hour suicide watch where there was a nurse's aide with me at all times. I had to keep the bathroom door open, even if it was a male aide tending to me while I went to the bathroom or showered. However, they did allow me to visit with Kyle for about an hour each day, albeit under a watchful eye of my nurse's aide. Kyle was still on life support and it was hard to tell if there was any change in his condition over the past week. All I knew was I wanted us to both go home.

During the days I was on 24-hour suicide watch, I spoke very little to anyone. I spent most of my time in deep meditation, listening to high vibration meditation music on my laptop. Also doing deep breathing exercises; I stayed present in the NOW moment, not allowing my mind to wonder. I refused any medication that was offered to me by nurses. They wanted me to take medication for hypertension; I guess my blood pressure was high. I have been completely holistic since 1998 and I would never take medication for high blood pressure. I know the best way to lower my blood pressure is naturally. I had cure myself many years ago from severe migraine headaches, simply by drinking more water and meditating daily.

It was December 14, 2011, exactly one week after the doctors had asked me if they could take Kyle off life support. This was the day that changed my life forever. During my daily visit with Kyle, I got very close and leaned over to whisper into his ear, "Kyle, get better so we can both go home." That night in a semi-sedated state Kyle pulled out the ventilator tube from his throat and then his feeding tube. He literally took himself off life support! Kyle's vital signs were excellent. A few days later, Dr. Ty, Kyle's intern, said to me, "His vital signs are so good it's like he was never even sick!" What Kyle and I both experienced was a true medical miracle during the Christmas season that year. One of my favorite Christmas movies is "Miracle on 34th Street" and HUP is located on 34th Street in Philadelphia. We experienced a true "Miracle on 34th Street" and we both went home on December 30, 2011, the day before New Year's Eve, and were able to celebrate the New Year together, at home.

There are no words that can express the gratitude I have in my heart and soul for being able to bring my son home. I know in my heart that I would not have been able to return home without him at that time in my life, and Spirit knew that as well. After experiencing that miracle, I made a promise that no matter what happens from then on, I'll never stop "Thanking God!" for allowing me to bring my son home and allowing me to celebrate a New Year with him here in the physical realm. That is a promise I have held true to ever since, and always will while I am here in this earthly realm.

I was blessed to be able to spend two and half more years with Kyle. During that time Kyle spent a lot of time with TJ my grandson, his nephew who was not quite two years old when he was in the hospital December 2011. I am so glad TJ got to know his uncle.

Kyle still being very young wanted to do all the things he used to be able to do before he got sick. It was hard for him not to do those things with his friends anymore. Even though I tried my best to get him to eat healthy, he would always sneak in fast food and pizza. He would just call up and have it delivered. He said to me "Ma, I can't do all the things I love to do, at least let me eat the foods I love." I didn't argue with him, yet I knew in my heart that eating those foods were not good for him and would eventually make him sicker.

On April 3, 2014, Kyle was having trouble breathing and I called for an ambulance. It was 27 months after I brought him home that fateful day in December 2011. Paramedics came quickly and he again walked down the stairs and to the ambulance on his own. Kyle always wanted to do as much as he could do physically for himself; he really pushed himself to keep on going even though his body, especially his heart, was not up to the task.

As the ambulance was driving off taking him to the hospital in Wilkes-Barre PA, because that is where his team of cardiologist doctors were located, I was "Thanking God" for giving me almost three more years with my son. I had no idea what was going to happen this time. I wanted to bring him home again of course, I wanted to experience another miracle, however I didn't know if that would be the case this time. I had to just say "Thank You GOD" and knowing this time that all things happen in Perfect Divine timing and it is a Soul Plan that Kyle and I made before we came into this incarnation. Kyle was transferred back to HUP in Philadelphia the next day by ambulance this time; the weather was not conducive for a Medevac helicopter and he was not in critical condition on life support like he was when he had been originally Medevac to HUP in November of 2011.

We had just celebrated my grandson TJ's fourth birthday the weekend before this happened, at the Chinese Buffet. Kyle drove his own car and met us there. Kyle loved that car and he had just bought it a few months before. My daughter Neukeyia, Kyle, TJ and I had a wonderful weekend together. But I wonder now if Kyle really was not feeling as well as we all thought. He did not go to the movies with us and that was unusual for Kyle, because he loved going to the movies and spending time with his nephew TJ.

Kyle was in the hospital for three months and he was only on life support the last month; he was put on life support after his open-heart surgery on May 28, 2014. Kyle's heart was getting weaker and weaker and he was rushed into surgery on the Wednesday morning after Memorial Day 2014. That is when Kyle asked me to call my brother to come wait with me, because he did not want me waiting in the surgical waiting room alone. I had never told Kyle about my suicide attempt the last time he was on life support. But somehow, he instinctively knew, and he did not want a repeat of that situation. I waited in the waiting room by myself and tried to get some rest, but sleep was not in the cards for me. The surgery was over nine hours and the young surgeon came to me and told me the surgery went very well. Once they had Kyle moved to an ICU room, I went to his side, and seeing him on life support again brought up all those memories from December 2011; it was heartbreaking for me to see Kyle on life support again. My hopes were that he would be off life support in a few days, because the surgery had gone well.

That was not to be the case. Even though the surgery initially went very well, there were complications a week later that led to an embolism bursting in his head. Once that happened doctors asked me again if they could take Kyle of life support, as they did not think he was going to make it through that trauma. I did not agree at first, and he was on life support for a month longer. Finally, after being by his bedside for the last month of his life here in the physical realm, I did agree to let them take him off life support. Because I knew he was no longer here; that was on July 1, 2014, the day he transitioned to spirit.

I was at complete peace when Kyle transitioned for three reasons. First because I KNEW he was not going anywhere; he would always still be with me. Second, I also KNEW it was his soul's time to return to spirit. No soul comes into this world before their time and no soul leaves this world before their time. All things are in Perfect Divine Timing; there are no accidents. And thirdly I KNEW it was a Soul Agreement he and I both had made together. It was his time to leave this earthy realm and I had more work to do here.

Caroline Chang, Tobyhanna, PA

Caroline Chang is the Producer and Host of Awake 2 Oneness Radio, Founder of The KYLE Foundation (Keep Your Light Expanding), and Co-Founder of Universal Oneness Alliance. She was inspired to launch her podcast six months after her son Kyle transitioned to spirit. Her mission is to inspire the world to awaken to the Universal Truth of Oneness. Spirituality and Science are teaching us we are literally all connected, we are all ONE and when Humanity awakens to this Truth there will be peace on earth.

TEXT MESSAGES FROM BEYOND THE VEIL

By Teresa L.

I've been texting my son that passed in October, it's been just a few short months and forever ago since he died, and I just needed to know he was alright. He was a good man with a problem, and he thought he could control it, but in the end, it took him.

I had him in my teenage years, and basically we grew up together. I miss him, and my continuing to text him feels normal because I believe that souls on the Other Side can read our messages. I find comfort in sending him my thoughts and feelings just like we always did.

A few days ago, before falling into a needed nap... I sleepily asked my son if he was reading the messages I've been sending him. I am not sure how long I had been asleep, but I woke from the most awesome dream!! A CONFIRMATION!! I saw my son sitting in his favorite recliner at our house, looking at a cell phone and smiling while nodding his head saying... "Yes, mom, I read them!" He looked happy... it did feel very real. I knew I had a dream visitation from him to let me know he is OK and to confirm that they can and do hear us.

I wanted to share that our loved ones are just beyond the veil.

Teresa L.

Arizona

Saving Grace

I'm passing sleeping cities

fading by degrees

and believing all I see to be so

I'm flying over backyards

country homes and ranches

watching life between the branches

below

Tom Petty

Chapter Fourteen

VICARIOUS DEATH BED MOMENTS

Dedicated to Those Who Stayed

I write to honor those who stayed
in that uncomfortable space
baring witness
to someone in agony
who smells funny
who is saddled with guilt and regrets
or is not themselves
or the person that they knew

Death is not necessarily pretty
but if you can sit
in its sacred fulfillment
offering nothing more
than the service of your presence
it is an amazing gift
both given and received

Claudia Watts Edge
Hospice volunteer

TWO LESSONS I LEARNED AS A

CHAPLAIN, FROM OTHERS' DEATHS

By Rev. Dr. Lee Witting

M any folks who have listened to my podcast, NDE Radio, or read my NDE-based novel, Beneath the Phoenix Door, have already encountered the story of my NDE at age seven, when I drowned in a lake in New Jersey. I hardly realized at that age how much it would change the direction of my life, even to the point of leading to a doctorate in near-death studies, and becoming a hospital chaplain. In that career, it was natural for me to focus on assuring the many patients who coded into an NDE that, rather than being crazy, they had experienced a great gift from the Light.

Being a chaplain, it goes without saying, is not a one-way street. Like all professionals working in life and death situations, chaplains will be caught up in both the painful and the miraculous in dealing with the reality of death and the hereafter. To that point, I'd like to share here the stories of two of my patients who did not recover, but instead involved me profoundly in their deaths. I call these very rare, very different stories my saddest and happiest examples of how to die, and how I believe I helped, and was helped, in turn.

First, the saddest:

Along with his family, I was attending the last throes of a man dying from a terribly painful cancer. Despite the painkillers, he cried out with anger and fear, thrashing in his bed despite the pleas and cries of his wife and the sobs of his children. He was determined not to die, he would not go peaceful into that good night, and his moans and swearing radiated beyond his family and staff to all the other patients in the unit.

Finally, as his soul fled his disease-ridden body, he spotted me, the only person in the room he was not related to. I felt his soul try to enter me, and suddenly I was overcome with an icy-cold nausea. I felt his soul's fear and confusion as I excused myself and stumbled out into the hall. Leaning against the wall, I pulled myself together enough to say, "You do not belong here, and you cannot stay. But look! There are friends and angels all around you who will help guide you into the Light. Ask for their help, and I know they will." And then I said a prayer for him. And with that, I felt his soul leave my body.

The intrusion I felt that day happened only once in the fifteen years and thousands of deaths I attended, but in many ways I felt it was my finest hour as a chaplain. I knew who I was, where he was, and the way death is structured – and I was able to point him in the right direction.

And then the happiest:

The miracle of a shared death experience of a very different sort. Again, I was in the room of a dying man, along with his family, but this time, the room was filled with love. Four generations attended this well-loved great-grandfather, who slept but surely heard the prayers and conversation of the family members, from his son to his infant great-grandchild. All of them were saying to him, in words or with their eyes, "We love you, granddad, we love you, and we'll be okay. Don't worry about us – we'll be fine, and we'll be with you again soon. We love you, we love you, we love you."

At the moment of his death, I saw – or rather, felt – the most amazing golden light flow down like honey into the room. It was the most perfect embodiment of God's love, beyond imagination, coming down into this humble hospital room to take the man home, and I was privileged to share in the glory of it. The gift I received that day was beyond any deserving, but I've held it as a prize to share with all the chaplains and hospice workers who find amazement in the presence of death

Rev. Dr. Lee Witting served for fifteen years as chaplain at Eastern Maine Medical Center. He earned a doctorate in near-death studies at Bangor Theological Seminary, and was editor of IANDS magazine "Vital Signs", before founding NDE Radio, a podcast where several hundred interviews with NDErs may be heard. His NDE-based novel, Beneath the Phoenix Door, what he terms 'adventure theology', is available through Amazon.

DAD AND DAUGHTER SHARED

DEATH EXPERIENCE

REAL SPIRIT CAUGHT ON CAMERA!

By Janet Tarantino

As a three-time near-death experiencer, end-of-life encounters, death, and the afterlife have fascinated me, so I started studying all aspects of these subjects by collecting accounts for additional books. The first book, titled DYING TO SEE Revelations About God, Jesus, Our Pathways, and the Nature of The Soul, was about my transcendental NDEs, STEs, and what I learned.

When my parents could no longer live alone, I happily stepped in to assist them until their end-of-life occurred, which took five years. I always knew, in my heart, that I was going to do this. Caregiving provided a fantastic opportunity to know my parents as people, even as friends, instead of merely my parents. I do not doubt that if we had been born in the same period, we would have been best friends. My parents read my book's manuscript over the five years as it morphed and turned into the book—now published. They also read the other fantastic NDE accounts I had collected for another book. These incredible celestial stories gave them comfort and peace that they would indeed never die.

Because I was with them so extensively, it gave me the perfect opportunity to study the dying process. So, I asked my parents if they would share everything they sensed, felt, saw, or experienced, on their trek to eternity, and they agreed. They also permitted me to share their accounts if they would be helpful, and they signed contracts stating this.

Over this period, I seemed to have developed a special bond with my dad and often felt his physical ailments. Here are a couple of examples. During an annual eye doctor appointment, I noticed a pain in my knee while waiting for the physician to enter. Immediately I thought of dad, who was having trouble walking due to bad knees. After the eye appointment, I stopped at the local sports shop, picked him up a new knee brace, and then headed to their place. I was astounded and surprised to see dad already clothed in his jacket, standing in a bent-over with his cane in hand, wanting to purchase a knee brace. I held up the knee brace like a grand prize, and I could visibly see a sense of relief wash over his entire body. He immediately headed to his reclining chair and sat down, still with his coat on, to slip the brace onto his leg.

Another instance of our connection occurred on a separate occasion when I dropped a friend off at the airport after he had come to visit. I was driving back home to their place and noticed I was having trouble seeing. The road signs were blurred so that I could not see them clearly. I considered pulling off the road, but I persisted because I needed to get home to help mom and dad. I immediately called the eye doctor for an appointment. Mom was sitting at the table with me when I made the call, and she asked me if I would make an appointment for dad. I managed to set our appointments up reasonably close together.

My appointment was first. Expecting to hear bad news, I was dumbfounded to hear my eye tests showed my vision had not changed, but when dad had his eye test done next, he could not see even the most enormous letters. Dad ended up needing laser corrective measures done to clear up his vision. So once again, it was dad's physical limitations I was feeling. I seemed to pick up these abilities after my most in-depth NDE when I met God and Jesus, and saw the nature of our soul. I also saw angels and more as described in the book.

My dad and I had a hoot of a time together. Some days he felt young again, so he would try to walk without his walker, and I would then hear a thump; he had fallen. I would hurry in and find him sitting on the floor. I check him over to make sure he was okay. Then he would remain sitting on the floor against the sofa, telling me not to worry about him. Well, of course, that is not going to happen! I sat on the floor next to him and would ask, "So what is happening down here?"; "How's the carpet looking?;" "Got a deck of cards?"; or some other ridiculous question. He would start laughing, and we sat on the floor just visiting until he felt ready for me to help him into his chair.

As a preface, I would like to mention, Dad had started wanting to go home, and he wanted the entire family to go along. In his mind, he wanted to take a trip back to his hometown in Iowa. He would ask if his van was working and if it was maintained. He also wanted to make sure he had wheels, so he asked if my car was in good repair for back-up purposes. I answered his inquiry by telling him I had a new car, and it was working correctly. However, it was not his home in Iowa that he wanted; it was his home in heaven that he was desiring.

Finally, when dad became confined to bed, I would frequently sit next to his bedside, and we would watch television together. In particular, one evening comes to mind because he casually was looking toward the corner of the room and said, "It's interesting to see mom is so well-traveled." Surprised at what my ears heard, my eyes opened wide, and I asked him, "Do you see grandma?" Dad responded by pointing toward the corner of the room and said, "Yes, I do. She's over there at the airport."

I mentioned to dad that maybe grandma had come to take him home as he had been wanting, and he nodded his head. The evening wore on; dad asked for his glasses because he was having trouble seeing the flight monitor. He was waiting for grandma's flight number to come up, but it never did. I explained to him that if he were supposed to take that flight that night with grandma, everything would become straightforward and easy to read. He agreed. In any case, grandma had merely stopped in to check on her son that evening, and that is how I explained it to him, and he agreed. He described her as looking young again. It was a beautiful experience to have witnessed.

Eventually, even with the combined help of my brother Dennis, his wife Judy, and my sister Diane, we could no longer provide the extensive care our parents needed, so we placed them into an excellent caregiving facility. They were doing well, for 90 years old, so I took a trip out of the country to see the love of my life. While I was away, I received news that my dad's death was imminent, but international travel does not happen fast, so I was unsure if I would make it.

I remembered the near-death experiences I had and remembered that we are energetic beings, and even though the human body has limitations, the spirit does not. So I went to bed that night, and in my imagination, I called out to dad. I inquired, "Dad! Dad! Are you there?" Fantastically I heard his reply. He said, "Yes, I'm here." I asked him, "Am I going to make it in time?" He answered, "It will be close, but I'll try."

The next morning, I called the airline to make arrangements, knowing I would make it in time and obviously, heaven must have had its fingers in the planning. I could get a ticket the next morning, which is unheard of! Usually there are no tickets available, or the prices are so high most people could not afford them. However, there was a seat available, and it was affordable too. I packed and frantically rushed to be with him. Everything worked like clockwork. I made the first connection, effortlessly flying into Denver, CO, to catch a connecting flight to Boise. However, fantastically the arriving flight had landed an hour early, again, which is unheard of, allowing me to catch an earlier flight to Idaho.

I notified Judy my sister-in-law, of the new arrival time, and she said she would be waiting. We loaded the luggage, and off we went. I was not only worried about my dad, but I was also worried about my mom. She was about to lose the man she had spent her entire life with, and I could not fathom what she must have been going through. I do not doubt that God had his fingers in the transportation arrangements, and I was able to spend the last seven hours with him. It also allowed all of us children to be there to say good-bye and support my mom in her hour of loss.

As Judy and I raced down the highway as fast as we could, we started receiving text messages from my sister Diane, who was with mom and dad at the facility. The texts read, "Hurry! He's failing!" Then a second "Where are you? Hurry!" I told my sister-in-law about my communique with dad about whether I would make it in time, and I shared with her his answer that it would be close, but he'd try. We chuckled a little, both confirming this would undoubtedly qualify.

After we arrived, we hurried to their unit so that I could spend some time with dad. They had described dad as being unresponsive. However, Mom asked dad twice if he knew I was there. The second time she asked, dad groaned, indicating that he did know I had arrived. I talked to him even though he did not answer, but I knew he was in there until he seemed to rest. I also set up my phone so he could listen to his favorite church music.

Diane had helped mom to bed because she needed some rest too, but she soon opened her eyes and wanted to sit with dad and hold his hand. We managed to get her into her wheelchair, securing her with a scarf to help support her, and took her to dad's side. She sat beside dad's bed and told him how much she loved him while patting the hand she held like a valuable treasure she never wanted to let go of. All of a sudden, mom cried out, "I'm dying! I'm dying too!" as she crumpled over. We caught her and quickly pulled the cord to notify the nursing staff we needed assistance. The help arrived. The nurse and Diane lifted mom into her bed and attended to her while I sat with my dad. After that, Diane stayed with mom, and I stayed with dad. Mom quickly fell to sleep and never saw dad again.

When the nurse stepped over to check dad after attending to mom, she reported his vitals had fallen a little. I believe, in hindsight, my mom must have felt my dad withdrawing his energetic link to her heart because he would be passing over soon. I truly believe my mom and my dad had a heart to heart connection, which was why she felt she was dying.

When we initially organized and decorated their apartment unit at the facility, mom and dad both said they only wanted one thing—they always wanted to see each other. Therefore, when the room was hard to maneuver in due to all the care equipment crowding the room. The decision was made, due to dad's unresponsiveness, to resituate dad into the living room. When the bed was repositioned into the new room, their one request to see each other was considered, so dad's bed was situated so he could quickly look down the bed's length and see mom resting in her bed in the other room.

Night fell. Both mom and dad were resting peacefully, so Diane and I decided to nap too. After all, having traveled 17 hours and not sleeping well the night before I left because of the news I had received, I was tired. Despite the lack of sleep, I woke up at 1:30 am, not long after drifting off, and felt the need to start recording videos. I believe it was dad's spirit who had woke me and it was dad's spirit who had nudged me to take the videos.

Later, when viewing the film, I was stunned to see I had captured dad's spirit zipping out of his body when he exhaled his last breath. Diane and I showed the video to our mom. She smiled and did not doubt that it was indeed him.

After Dad transitioned, both my sister and I stayed with our mom every moment of every day. Two days after dad departed, mom was lying in the recliner. I heard her say something, but I could not hear her clearly, so I asked what she said. She replied, "I'm singing to the song. Don't you hear it?" I answered, "No, I don't hear it." Mom and I both started looking around the room to discover where the song might be coming from, but even though I could not hear it, she could. Out of curiosity and a little bit of knowledge, I asked my mom what the song's name was. She answered the inquiry with "It's—Good Night Sweetheart."

Remembering that my dad would often enter the living room in the morning, sing a few lines of a song, get down on his knees next to her while she sat in the recliner, then he would lean over to kiss her good morning, I knew, without a doubt, this must have been him who was singing to her, and only she could hear it. My face cracked in a huge smile, and I told mom, "That has got to be dad!" She smiled and agreed.

Mom ended up transitioning nine days after dad did. As her final time came closer, she reported seeing friends from high school and dead family members. On her final days, she saw the more important people in her life, like my brother, who had died unexpectedly of a massive heart attack in his early 60s.

Also, before mom left this world, she reported seeing into heaven and she said, "It's so beautiful! Animals are roaming free together, beautiful fields, clean streets, some white buildings, and some orange buildings. It's just so beautiful!" I was adjusting the sheets and blankets up behind her head at the time. She tilted her head back and exclaimed, "I really see it, Jan, I really do see it." I told her that I had no doubt she did.

The night before mom became unresponsive, we knew she saw dad because she exclaimed, "Dick!" Dick was my dad's name. I asked her, "You see dad? What does he look like?" She grinned the biggest smile, and she answered, "He looks sooo sharp!" It was not long after that that mom transitioned too. Mom and dad had always said they would walk into heaven hand in hand, and we did not doubt that dad had come back to take her hand so they could walk into heaven together like they always said they would.

After their transition and our return to our family homes in different states, I created the film of my dad's efforts of providing video proof telling this story and featuring the film of his spirit whipping out of his body. It is 13 minutes, entitled REAL SPIRIT CAUGHT ON CAMERA.

My dad was always an honest man and a man of his word. I have no doubt letting me capture his spirit leaving his body was my dad's last effort to share with me, and the world, what he was experiencing during his dying process.

I was even more shocked when I saw in the movie Real Spirit Caught On Camera that a ball of light swoops down into the film's upper left video frame just as I say, Dick, my dad's name. It is easiest to see it on a larger screen device like a laptop. It was as if, dad was watching me create the video and was making his movie debut by confirming he is flying alive and free and will be ever-present until we meet again.

YouTube Video Hyperlink:

https://www.youtube.com/watch?v=m8fWTuoMyRY&t=5s

Special note: There was no television in dad's room and no electrical equipment on in his room except for his hospital bed plugged into the wall. There were no windows in his room because it was an interior room, and there were other units on either side of mom and dad's unit. The window shades were closed for the evening in the other room, and due to my parents' need for high-level care, their unit was in the back of the building where there was no street or parking area. A high privacy fence surrounded that area of the building. So there could not possibly have been an outside light that might have caused this phenomenon. It was my dad's real spirit leaving his body that I had captured, and it was similar to the blue color of my spirit that I saw in my most in-depth NDE. This video called Real Spirit Caught On Camera is available on the Janet Tarantino YouTube channel.

Janet is an NDE Speaker, NDE Researcher, Author, Host of her own YouTube channel, blogger, previous Senior Caretaker, Inventor, a better mother, and a better friend. For more information on Janet Tarantino, go to: Email: JanetTarantinoauthor@gmail.com

https://www.facebook.com/JanetTarantinoNDEr/

https://www.instagram.com/janettarantino_author/

https://www.youtube.com/channel/UCj1CQ6FU3SiCEI6Bt8-Ou9g

https://www.janettarantino.com/

DO YOU SEE THEM?

Excerpt from the book 'TRANSITIONS' A nurse's education about Life and Death.

By Becki Hawkins

When I was working for the big city hospital's brand-new hospice I was visiting the cutest little Pentecostal minister you've ever seen. He had a shock of white hair and bright baby blue eyes. He lived next door to his church built in the '50s and surrounded with ancient oaks.

He lived with his second wife Matilda. She called him 'the Reverend Smith' since she was one of his parishioners before his first wife died, and thought it was disrespectful to call him by his first name.

Matilda liked to stay in the kitchen when I came to visit, but I tried to get her to listen to all I was saying to her husband about hospice. She would flap her flowered full-bodice apron, turn on her heels and run off again.

On day while sitting at my desk at work, the receptionist leaned around my cubicle and said, "Hey Florence {that's what she called all the nurses} that lady that calls and screams about her husband needing help just called and said to hurry on over there."

I called her to reassure her that I was on my way and tried to repeat the info we had gone over. I told her to call her next-door neighbor and see if she would come and be with them till I got there.

When I arrived, my sweet patient was sitting straight up in his trusty rocking recliner struggling for air with a serious color of blue taking over his face. "Can you get me to bed? I want to see out that picture window."

I picked him up and carried him to his quilt-covered bed and straddled him, holding him up as straight as I could so he could breathe better. Matilda ran back into the kitchen with her face in her apron and the neighbor ran home.

Dear brother Smith patted my fingers on his left shoulder.

"Do you see them?" He gasped with excitement.

"No, sir, but tell me. What are you seeing?" I whispered back into his ear.

"The room here is now full of angels."

"Tilda, come quick! I've got to go now. I'll see you again Honey... later on."

He tried to comfort her. Off she went again to her safety net.

He lifted up his right hand into the air and called out, "My Lord. My Lord and my God." And then he fell back against me with his last breath.

I just sat there for several moments until Tilda came back into the living room, surprisingly calm now. She helped me lay his head down on his feather pillow and I held her awhile. She didn't run away anymore.

Some say it's a lack of oxygen, some say it's due to pain medication or organ failure.

Me? I'm proud I got to be there.

Becki Hawkins,

Oklahoma, Author of the book 'TRANSISTIONS' a nurse's education about life and death. She has recently retired as an oncology and hospice nurse, hospice Chaplin, newspaper columnist, and shares her experiences nationwide as a speaker to other professionals in the field of oncology and hospice care.

FLOATING KLEENEX

By Claudia Watts Edge

It has been almost a month of hospitalization for my sweet mother Lillian. Together we must face the dissolving hope that the mountain she has been endlessly climbing will ever level off. There will be no summit or personal flags planted at the top in celebration of her returning good health. The boulder she has been pushing uphill is beginning to slip as gravity has turned into an unrelenting downward spiral.

My job throughout her stay has been the fulfillment of an unspoken contract. I am to remain at her side and witness the decline, the 'hard fight' of her will and resilience, as her ability to bounce back is fading into the sunset. I stay here day and night to assist in what remains of her independence, an oxymoron I know, but the trust is deep set between us, and I am happy in my duty of seeing to her dignity and helping keep the decorum of modesty in the middle of the bed bathing and bed panning.

The trust of what is best to do, and what she will no longer do, has been handed solely to me.

She looks to me now when the doctor comes into the room and the freight train begins to run through her head. She can no longer listen to any more advice of the next steps or of treatments to be ordered. We are all in varying stages of resignation to the inevitable.

That night in the dark, as I lay in the familiar padded nook below the window contemplating the day's events, I had a clear vision.

I had grown used to a familiar routine of how her left hand stayed clutched around the hospital tissue box. Every few minutes she would pull out a folded fresh tissue with her right hand, bringing it up to her mouth to cough, and then let the used tissue drop to the floor to be collected later in the garbage. This motion had gone on for weeks, the swooshing sound of the tissue being pulled out of the box, then the coughing jag, and then the drop of the balled up soiled tissue to the floor. I heard it day and night, and there was no need to rise now to look and see what these noises meant, because I knew them by heart,

SWOOSH, COUGH... COUGH... COOUUGHH... WAD... DROP.

But the vision showed me an entirely different scene as the neatly folded tissue was pulled from the box, SWOOSH, COUGH... COUGH... COOUGHH... WAD, but... it did not softly drop to the floor this time, as she released it. Instead, the tissue defied gravity, and floated upwards toward the ceiling in the softest of motions. Watching it lift upward like a silent white dove, I knew I had just received a sign, a gentle certainty that her time was coming to an end, and that she too would soon be rising out of the restrictive box that held her spirit.

The rest of the story holds the personal acts and decisions made about anxiety reducing doses of morphine, and the doubts that arise after those hard decisions are made. One cannot help but second guess everything afterwards. Did I do enough, did I ease her pain, and was there another treatment I should have tried before letting her go?

I am comforted in the answers to those questions now, but in the middle of loss and grief, the doubts are tangible. But I take comfort in the vision I was gifted the night before her passing, the beautiful message sent to me of her upcoming release, in the form of a soft white tissue that floated toward the sky.

Claudia Watts Edge, West Jordan, Utah, is the Author of GIFTS FROM THE EDGE Stories of the Other Side, and Volume II Lessons from the Other Side. She is a Popular Speaker, and Light Worker. Find interviews, podcasts and a full biography, or contact Claudia on her website claudiaedge.com

Chapter Fifteen

HEALING THROUGH MUSIC
AND OTHER HEAVENLY THERAPIES

THE ART OF THE JOURNEY

Who is it that looks back at me
this weathered one
reflected in the mirror

I gaze in retrospect of my life as work of art
the wrinkles are the imprint of my journey
a road map of smiles and tears
that have carved a path
around the mouth that laughed and sang
and kissed lovers and babies

I am not old
I am rare
I am not waiting to die
I am in the fullness of my existence

Ask me to dance

Claudia Watts Edge

HEAL-U

One Woman's Journey to Overcome Incurable Cancer

By Jenny Kennedy

One sentence. That's all it took. One sentence and my body shut down. Immediately. Entirely. "I'm so sorry, you have incurable ovarian cancer." I didn't hear another word the doctor said. I couldn't talk. I couldn't walk. I sat motionless with one thought in my head: I'm going to die.

How long the doctor spoke, I have no idea. My body and mind were elsewhere. Finally, I was jolted back to reality. "I will get you a wheelchair so you can take Jenny to your car." No! There was no way I was going to be put in a wheelchair. Mustering all my strength I pulled myself out of my seat and, with the supporting arm of my husband, slowly made my way to our car. I had arrived at the doctor's surgery concerned but still feeling healthy and optimistic, with a spring in my step. I left like an old lady barely able to walk.

Forming the belief that I would die had had an immediate and drastic impact on my body. I was, indeed, far closer to death than when I had arrived. It is somewhat ironic then that an understanding of the physical effect of those words would ultimately form the basis of my healing. But I didn't know it. Not yet.

I had worked professionally as an Intuitive Healer and Massage Therapist for ten years prior to my diagnosis, and had done a lot of personal development and healing on myself. I couldn't believe I ended up with a diagnosis of incurable cancer and I felt a lot of shame as I had professed to be able to heal others, but hadn't healed myself. At the time of my diagnosis in December 2012 I looked and felt healthy, but I had noticed a lump in my lower abdomen. I wasn't too concerned. I thought it was just a fibroid. Cancer never ever entered my mind. In hindsight there were other symptoms, but I had put them down to menopause. This is why ovarian cancer is known as "the silent killer." It is not usually diagnosed until the later stages.

After the diagnosis, shock gradually turned into terror and I shook like a leaf from sunup to sundown. Sleep was intermittent and fitful. My mind had only one thing on it. I didn't want to share the news with those closest to me as I wanted to spare them the worry, but I knew I would be unable to hide the truth from them. So it was with a heavy heart that I shared my news with my loved ones. I had never wanted to be a burden and cause grief to anyone. Then, ten days following my diagnosis I was abruptly woken early one morning to a voice in my head telling me that I was healed. This wasn't just wishful thinking. It was a palpable relief and knowing that flooded my body. I liken it to the feeling a mother would have if her child were lost in the bush. Searchers are scouring everywhere as her anxiety grows with every passing hour. Then her phone rings with the news her child has been found. She hasn't yet laid eyes on her child, but she knows it will be only a matter of time before she does.

I didn't yet know how I would heal but I KNEW I would.

Because of my profession I had a highly developed intuition and I believe, when I was in fear from the diagnosis and facing a life and death situation, my reptilian brain (where our automatic self-preserving behavior patterns that ensure our survival originate) took over from my thinking mind. That voice in my head was my intuition guiding me. In my journey of healing I uncovered six steps to healing which I call HEAL-U. This was my first step.

H – Hope and Believe.

In the weeks following my diagnosis, people rang and visited. Some of these connections were helpful and some were destructive. When I conveyed the news to my spiritual friends, they almost jokingly said "You'll get this sorted. You have the skills and knowledge to heal – this is just part of the plan."

On hearing these words my confidence grew and I believed in my ability to heal. However, one friend came to visit me and told me of another woman who had just been given the same diagnosis as me... but she had died. I was astounded that my friend would even consider conveying this news to me. Immediately I felt my body constrict with fear. However, that friend did me a great favor. I decided then and there to become discerning about who I would share my journey with. I would only surround myself with people who believed I could heal. I have since come to understand that once you have set an intent or said a prayer the Universe will always work FOR you. I had set the intent to heal and everything that took place in my life, whether perceived as good or bad, was an opportunity for me to move one step closer to manifesting that intent. My friend had given me an opportunity to take that one step closer. This was my second step to healing.

E – Encouragement and Support.

I believed I could heal. I was surrounded by people who believed I could heal. They encouraged and supported me. But how was I going to do it? I knew of no formula I could follow. I had no option other than to follow my intuition. And, when I doubted my intuition, I would ask the Universe for signs to confirm what I believed to be the right path.

The body is the barometer to the soul, so I decided to ask my body for an answer. I set this intention and then went into meditation. I closed my eyes and allowed myself to take some gentle breaths as my body relaxed. As I intuitively scanned my body, I was drawn to one of the tumors. I could "see" it as a foreign object in a perfect body. Growing and pushing its way out. In my mind I "asked" it why is it here and what has it come to teach me? Surprisingly, these words sprang into my awareness.

"You look good Jenny; you feel great, but you are out of alignment with your soul. You are not listening and living from your authentic self. The veneer is cracking as the truth tries to come to the surface. Follow the signs your body gives you and you will heal." And this became my third step to healing.

A – Aware of Your Inner Knowing.

I shared what I had uncovered with a good friend Jude, who had undertaken training similar to mine. I invited her to come over and hold space for me as I got to the root cause of what had created this cancer. I wanted to know where I had stepped out of alignment with who I really was. My husband, on the other hand, didn't really get it. He was an engineer and found it difficult to understand the concept of what I was doing. However, that didn't stop him from encouraging and supporting me to do whatever I needed to and felt right for me.

Jude and I settled ourselves down in the sacred space of my warm and cozy healing room We offered up a prayer to both be guided during meditation, to help me uncover the root cause. We asked for whatever needs to happen to take place, in order for me to heal. I closed my eyes as Jude gently guided me down ten steps. Inviting me to relax and surrender into the unknown with each step I took. When I reached the bottom step, she encouraged me to enter through a special door, one that would unlock the key to my healing.

As I entered a scene began to unfold in front of me. I couldn't see it completely, but I could sense it and a strong musky smell filled my nostrils. I waited for a moment as I could feel fear, shame and guilt beginning to rise up from the depths of my being. I was being held in a dungeon, chained to a post. There were three younger people with me also chained up. We were all petrified. I was in Switzerland back in the 1500s and I was a witch, doing what I do now. Witches, in those days, were held responsible for natural disasters and I was being used as a scape goat. The three younger people were my under-studies. My punishment was to watch them get burnt at the stake before it was my turn. As this scene unfolded my emotions became stronger. Tears streamed down my face as relief engulfed my whole body. Lifetime upon lifetime of anxiety, fear, feelings of abandonment, and myriad other suppressed emotions surfaced to be released. In that moment I GOT IT! The revelation of this past life uncovered a life transforming (and saving) realization.

It isn't my fault. I am innocent.

In that lifetime I was only trying to help and heal others but, not only did I lose my life, I also caused the death of others.

Jude then gently asked me to cut what is known as energetic cords and attachments to that lifetime, and when I felt this had been completed she guided me back up the stairs and invited me to open my eyes when I was ready. Upon opening my eyes we looked at each other in wonderment and Jude gave me a great big hug. We then discussed how I had also carried these beliefs into this lifetime. I had been emotionally, physically, and sexually abused and had a deep-seated belief (which up until that point I was unaware of) that somehow, I was to blame. I must have done something wrong to deserve these abuses. My guilt and shame played out in this lifetime by making me a chronic people pleaser, a high achiever – doing anything I could to feel good and find love, anything to prove that I was okay and not flawed. Throughout my life I believed that I wasn't good enough, even though on the outside it looked like I had everything together.

I tried so hard to be the best at everything. The best at every sport I played, the best wife, mother, friend, housekeeper, cook and employee. Everything I did was driven from the fear of not being good enough. I over gave to my own detriment. Ten years before my cancer diagnosis I had burnt out in the corporate world. Uncovering this past life not only released suppressed emotions that had built up over many years, but it allowed me to finally get angry. Many people said to me, "I can't believe you got cancer; you are so nice." Well, that is exactly why I got cancer. I had stuffed that anger down, ignored my soul and my own needs, and put others first.

As Dr Candace Pert, a cellular biologist and author, discovered and wrote in her book Molecules of Emotion, "Every time we suppress an emotion it physically gets stored in our cells. Over time there is the propensity to develop dis-ease where that suppressed emotion is stored."

No wonder I got ovarian cancer. Our ovaries are where we create life. I didn't know how to create a life for myself. I was out of touch with my own boundaries and needs. I was too busy quashing my needs in order to accommodate others. As a consequence of continually living in fear and trying to pre-empt things going wrong (because of the belief that it would be my fault) I lived constantly from a place of flight and fight. I had done this for so long that my body had forgotten how to activate my para-sympathetic nervous system, used to rest, digest, and restore. But even when I was supposedly resting, my para-sympathetic nervous system was still not activated so I was always feeling stressed. (I was clinically diagnosed with Post Traumatic Stress Disorder). It is through the breath that we can activate the para-sympathetic nervous system and I had to relearn how to breathe properly.

This is where true healing began for me. As I connected with the anger that arose and then asked myself what I was going to do about it, I began to learn to say NO, to speak my truth and to make decisions for myself. A common theme for the healing of victims of abuse is for them to have strong boundaries and take back the personal power that has been robbed from them.

Another gift that came from uncovering that past life took place for my son. I recognized him as one of my understudies in that lifetime. He had been struggling with drugs in this lifetime, and once again, that belief played itself out for me. I felt shame and guilt thinking I was to blame; I wasn't a good mother, and I must have done something wrong. I was living from a place of believing I would be responsible for his life and he could die, as had eventuated in that past life. We are energetically connected to our children and as I released this belief he began to heal and take responsibility for himself. I am so proud of the man he has now become. This was my fourth step to healing.

L – Led to the Root Cause.

Because the cancer was diagnosed in early December, no operation was possible until 4 January. During that time the tumor grew exponentially, to the extent that, when I lay down, there was a melon-sized lump protruding from my abdomen. I prayed and begged to be healed without surgery, but my intuition knew that this wasn't possible. Remember step one. For something to materialize you must first believe it. I didn't honestly believe that I could heal the cancer without some assistance from conventional medicine. Consequently, I had major surgery. I was extremely ill following my operation, and four days later I was informed that they wanted to do a gastroscopy, as stomach cancer was also suspected. Lying in my hospital bed on the morning of the procedure I was terrified. I just did not know how much my poor body could take. But I knew that our thoughts create our reality, so I summoned all my strength to turn those thoughts from fear to a place of trust.

I surrendered and said, "Okay GOD you take care of this." I refer here to the word GOD as an acronym of the Grand Order of Design (a phrase coined by the great Dr Wayne Dyer). My mind and body immediately became calmer as I saw myself handing over this worry.

As I was wheeled into theatre a doctor of Indian descent and dressed in his scrubs approached. He shook my hand and introduced himself. "Hello, I am Dr Shiva, and I will be looking after you today." I couldn't contain myself and burst out laughing. "If you are doing my procedure for me today, I will be fine." Shiva is a Hindu God and my prayer had literally been answered as I surrendered and handed over my concerns. GOD was taking care of me.

I knew at that point that I was being watched over in my journey of healing, and was being supported from all realms. I found out later that laughing produces endorphins that relax the esophagus and relieve pain, so I had no aftereffects from the gastroscopy. And the good news was, the cancer had not metastasized into my stomach. A few days later I was released from hospital to recover for six weeks before I was scheduled to begin chemotherapy.

The surgeon who performed the major abdominal surgery, for some unknown reason whenever she saw me, would always reiterate that she was unable to cure me. However, a couple of days following my hospital release, she phoned with my pathology results which confirmed what she had already suspected. The cancer was Stage 3C and supposedly incurable. As a parting shot, she once again said "I can't cure you" and then added "and you can't cure you BUT between the two of us I believe you are an A1 student." She knew I was following a spiritual path to healing. I took this as a sign that I was on the right path.

In fact, I received many signs that my intuition was guiding me to a place of wholeness and health. Any time I didn't totally trust my intuition, I surrendered and asked for a sign. I had had one-third of the recommended chemotherapy when I knew that I had had enough. My intuition told me, but fear and doubt crept in and overtook my inner belief. Waiting to see my oncologist and then go for another round of chemo, I once again surrendered and said to my grandmother in spirit, "Nanny I know I have had all the chemo I need. Can you please give me a sign that this is correct?" Immediately my attention was drawn to the television playing softly in the corner of the room and, to my astonishment, the words LIVING WELL were plastered across the screen in capital letters. This boosted my confidence no end, but I still wasn't completely convinced. I found it scary to go against what my oncologist was recommending. When I got in to see him, he informed me that my platelets were not recovering enough from the previous chemo and that they would have to cut the dosage significantly. I was relieved. This was another sign but still, I didn't have the courage to cancel the next infusion.

With my mind bouncing from fear to belief about whether my decision was right and that my journey with chemotherapy had come to an end, I eased myself into the treatment chair to receive the cocktail of chemicals that would supposedly prolong my life for a few more months. However, someone or something else had other plans for me. One nurse after another repeatedly jabbed me trying to find a vein to administer the chemotherapy. Finally, following five nurses' unsuccessful attempts I thought to myself, "If I don't believe it now, I never will. It's being made impossible for me to receive any more." I called an immediate halt to any further attempts. The flurry and panic of the medical staff could not disrupt my confidence and belief that my intuition was right, and I skipped down the corridor of that hospital knowing that life was about to get a whole lot better. This was my fifth step to healing

5– Let go and Surrender. If in doubt, hand your fears over and allow yourself to be guided.

There is also another aspect to this step of surrendering. Many people believe the way to healing is to think positive. However, this is unrealistic and unhealthy. There were times when I was fearful and doubted my ability to heal and when those instances arose, I would surrender to those feelings. Emotion is energy in motion and if we feel it fully it can then move through the body. I believe I had created cancer by not feeling my feelings. I certainly wasn't going to continue to do that. The trauma of my past experiences had been locked into my body and every time I acknowledged an emotion and changed the belief that was connected to that emotion, I was releasing the past as well as the present. This would then enable me to go forward and create a whole different future for myself.

I was searching through YouTube one day when I came across a scientist named Dr Bruce Lipton. He is a cellular biologist and the author of Biology of Belief. He had discovered that "It is the perception of the environment that controls a cell. In human terms perception is belief. It is our beliefs that control our cells." When we change a belief, we release suppressed emotions and reframe our mind and body. Not only have I physically healed from cancer, as I have learned to love myself, change my beliefs and listen to what is right for me, my relationships have grown, my wealth has grown, and I am living a life beyond my wildest dreams.

The last step to HEAL-U is

U – Unleash your Plan

This is where you create a plan to follow what feels right for YOU. When I created my plan, I felt like I had control and it gave me a job. This allowed me to step out of fear a lot more easily. It also boosted my immune system, and we all know that when our immune system is strong it gives the body the greatest opportunity to heal itself.

My plan involved:

Eating healthily which incorporated lots of fruit and vegetables and small portions of meat.

Swimming in the ocean and walking daily barefoot on the beach.

Qi Gong, which is an ancient Chinese exercise and healing technique that involves meditation, controlled breathing, and movement exercises. Sometimes I would have to do this lying down and visualizing it when I was very ill.

Dancing to music I loved which, at times, was merely my head moving as I "lost myself" to the sounds.

Making a conscious effort to be around positive and uplifting people.

Doing things that I enjoyed without allowing myself to get tired.

Regular massage.

And most importantly being true to myself and recognizing beliefs I hold that no longer serve me. This allows me to learn to love myself more and I believe LOVE is what heals us. The bonus is, when we love ourselves, we can live our lives to our fullest potential.

However, my story does not finish there.

It is a shame that some of us wait until we realize that our lives are finite to take stock and make changes. My husband and I were certainly guilty of that. We had been living in a small rural town that was cold in the winter. Neither of us liked the weather there, and we had been wanting change for a long time. We were warm climate people who loved the beach and water. So, we decided to up stakes and move from the South Island of New Zealand to the beautiful beachside town of Mount Maunganui in the North Island. Consequently, I had to be assigned a new medical team.

By this stage I had chosen not to have any more blood tests as I had decided I would not have any more chemotherapy. I had been told there was nothing more that could be done for me when cancer returned, except more operations to cut the cancer out to give me a little longer. I continued with my six-monthly check-ups simply to stay in the system to become a statistic; one of those who had beaten the odds. When I was first diagnosed, no one was able to give me any statistics on people who had survived and what they had done.

Here I was in the consulting room of my newly assigned gynecologist. He had just finished examining me when he said, "You need to have blood tests so that I can see where you are at with your cancer markers." I explained to him my position and said I was surprised it wasn't written down in my notes. His response was "Oh no, I need to see where your cancer markers are at." Once again, I reiterated my position.

Totally ignoring me he took out a laboratory form and began filling it in. Placing it on the desk in front of me he said "No, I need to know. Here is a form for you to take to the laboratory." Furiously I picked up that form and walked out of his office. Anger built up inside. I wasn't being listened to. NO seemed not to mean NO. I sat with that form for two whole days, then defiantly went off to the lab. "I'll show him" I thought. Ten days later as I was sitting at my office desk, the phone rang. It was my new MD (whom I had not yet met). "Has anyone rung to give you the results of your blood tests?" she asked. "No. "I replied. "Oh," she said, followed by a long awkward pause. "I am so sorry to tell you that your cancer markers have shot right back up. You will need to make an appointment with your oncologist as soon as possible." Then she hung up. I was in shock. This wasn't part of my plan. I believed I was healed. What had gone wrong? Five minutes later the phone rang once more. My MD must have had second thoughts as she informed me that she was here for me if I needed to talk.

I made that appointment with my oncologist and, in the meantime, also decided I would talk to my new MD. With the wind knocked out of my sails, I sat dejectedly in my MD's office as she went over the information that I had just filled out as a new patient. To my surprise she said to me "I see what you do for a job." As I had filled in

Intuitive Healer as my occupation. Why do you think your cancer markers have risen?" Thrilled to have chosen an MD who was on the same page as me I replied, "Because I haven't finished my healing yet." "Exactly," she responded.

I left her room knowing that I still had more healing to do. The only option my oncologist could give me was to begin chemotherapy straight away. I declined and informed him I would be back in three months' time for another blood test. During those three months I looked at how I had allowed a man (my gynecologist) to persuade me to go against my intuition. Why hadn't I simply taken that form and thrown it away. Why had I responded to him in such a way that he didn't respect my decision?

Three months later my cancer markers had dropped right back down again. Of course, my medical team was perplexed as to how that could happen. But I knew exactly. Remember I said the Universe is always working for you? Even though that wasn't part of my plan it was part of GOD's plan, as I now had medical evidence of what suppressing emotions can do and what happens when they are released. Suppressing emotions leads to chemical changes in the cells that, in turn, can lead to cancer. Releasing emotions relieves stress, boosts the immune system, and allows the body to heal naturally.

I was a woman who lived in fear. I now live in faith, peace, and love!

Jenny Kennedy, Mount Maunganui, New Zealand. She is an Intuitive Healer and Teacher (www.jennykennedy.co.nz) and works worldwide with clients both one on one and in workshops.

HEALING THROUGH MUSIC

By Ellen Whealton

Over thirty years ago, I suffered a traumatic brain injury when a horse kicked me in the temple. I was in a coma for about a week and what I experienced was nothing short of miraculous.

At first, I found myself on a wooden raft, floating on pink clouds. There were two guides with me on the raft. On the left was a young, thin bald man in brown robes. I later recognized him as a young Buddha. The guide in front of me was Jesus, who was wearing simple white robes. His eyes were pools of love and he communicated through his thoughts. I stood on the raft, aware of a warm, loving energy in pulling me towards it. I was being pulled to Heaven. I floated away from the raft, leaving all human existence behind, moving directly into my higher presence.

I found myself surrounded by bright, white light, with small glimpses of rainbow colors and breathtaking music. It was music that I had never heard before and have hot heard since. The instruments were unique and beautiful, and the music felt light, joyous, and celebratory. That didn't seem to last long, however, because soon the light expanded to encompass everything.

Then it became an experience of pure love.

Heaven wrapped me in love, seeping into my essence. I melted into it, becoming the love.

There was no worrying, no fear, no ego... "I" was gone and was replaced by love and powerful white light. There was no time in this place, but I left faster than I wanted to and somehow found myself back on the raft.

I was asked: "Do you want to live, or do you want to stay with us in Heaven?" Oddly, I remember struggling with the answer to this question. I wanted so much to stay in Heaven where I felt loved and whole. I knew everything would be alright, either way, but was given the gift of knowledge before I decided. I was only 12 at the time, but I remember being given great clarity and insight that stays with me to this day. It became clear that my passing would affect my family's ability to live out their purpose in this life. But there was something even greater that I knew I had to do in this lifetime, and that superseded everything else.

My life's purpose became crystal clear. I am meant to help heal people through music. In that moment, with the decision to live, my life truly began. To heal people with music. I felt overwhelmingly grateful at that moment and then moved into darkness again.

In the darkness, I could see colorful notes on a staff of music. I watched the notes dance along the staff, changing color with every move, moving closer to me as it did so. Finally, the music moved through me and I could hear the music, ever so slightly. It took every ounce of my concentration and strength to pull the sound of that music closer to me. I know now that I was being pulled back into my body through the music. The more I focused, the louder it became, until it resonated so powerfully in my head, it was booming. Then, all at once, the music stopped. It stopped as I opened my eyes. I was led back to my body through music.

Ellen Whealton,

Carlsbad CA

Ellen is a Near-Death Experiencer, light worker, transpersonal and music therapist, healer, workshop presenter and educator who uses numerous modalities such as music, sound bowls, essential oils, reiki and meditation in her practice. She is trained in the Bonny Method of Guided Imagery and Music, Holotropic Breathwork, Reiki, and Aroma-Release. She has an in-depth educational Facebook group called Music, Therapy & Essential Oils.

Ellen has a 12-episode series on the AwakeTV network and her work was recently highlighted by Jack Canfield, 42 times NYT bestselling author of the Chicken Soup books and The Success Principles in the forward of his newest book. Elements of her story can be found on several podcast interviews via Apple and on the Near-Death Experience YouTube channel.

Contact Ellen Email: wellnessmusictherapy@yahoo.com

THE JOURNEY OF A LIFETIME

By Sandra M. Champlain

Looking back through the last twenty-three years I cannot believe where I was and where I am now. Although there has certainly been suffering, grief and much heartache, those things have led me to a spiritual adventure that I would not trade for the world. In fact, I have come to believe that it is our suffering that can give birth to our unique spiritual discoveries and we can choose who we are and how we wish to live our lives.

My adventure began when I was thirty when I developed an incredible fear of death. My mind would constantly search for answers or try to fathom a time when I no longer existed. I worked full-time and had plenty of responsibilities, but when my mind was quiet a sense of dread about death and dying always crept in.

Although I call myself a skeptic, back then I was pretty arrogant and truly believed I knew the truth about mysticism and the afterlife. My thoughts were that you had to see it, hear it, touch it, smell it, or taste it to believe it was real. I honestly felt sorry for people who were overly religious, or who read books in the New Age section of a bookstore. As I may be embarrassed by the actions and beliefs of my younger self, I see now that I am the perfect person to tell this story.

Every so often in life a person comes along to be our friend, mentor or even angel in disguise. In my case I met a new friend named Nance, who was grounded as a dialysis nurse, but believed in topics like afterlife communication, spirit guides, angels, and an unseen world. At the time my fear had me studying major world religions, trying desperately to find some proof of the afterlife so my mind could be at peace. I was comforted to know that all the religions have a belief in life after death, but my fear still remained.

Nance took me to a medium doing a stage show demonstration one afternoon. I was astonished to hear such evidential words coming from the medium and it was clear from the reactions of the recipients that she was in fact somehow in communication with their deceased loved ones. I had to know more. Secretly I flew across the United States to study with this medium on a weekend course in mediumship.

At the beginning of the course she gave us the elements of evidential mediumship readings and how to conduct one. For strictly example purposes, she gave us each the assignment to pretend to be a medium and she would walk us though the elements. We were simply to make up that a person was standing behind our partner and tell the basics of what we saw, heard, and felt in our mind's eye. As I feel I am a creative person I confidently closed my eyes and told my partner of the person I pretended was standing behind her. When my turn was over and I opened my eyes, my partner had tears streaming from her face. Her grandfather was in fact named Jan, he lived in Denmark, worked as a fisherman and died of lung cancer. All words that I had spoken to her thinking I was making them up. My partner turned to me and correctly identified many things about my grandfather. That was the instant my fear of death dissipated and my belief into the world of the afterlife began.

Mediumship was good but I quickly learned that I was not always right. Very often my imagination produced people that were not the deceased loved ones of anyone. I have come to learn that you cannot become a good medium in a weekend. One must have a lifelong dedication to learning, sitting quietly to attune to the spirit world for "the power" and willing to be of service to others.

Through my years I have explored many topics including near-death experiences (NDEs), bedside visitations, signs from loved ones, reincarnation, induced after death communications (IADCs), spirit artists, evidential, physical and trance mediums, visual and auditory trans-communications including Electronic Voice Phenomena (EVP) and more.

One of the biggest moments for me happened while on a retreat at the Omega Center in Rhinebeck, New York. In the privacy of a cabin with only raindrops to record, I held out my digital recorder and asked my deceased loved ones to try to speak loudly if I were to believe that recording voices of those in the afterlife was real. When I played back the recording just prior to bedtime I heard two male and two female voices on my recording saying "Goodnight Sandra. Goodnight, goodnight, goodnight." As happy as I was I did have a difficult time sleeping that night! How close is this spirit world and are people always watching me? Lucky for me I found the book by Concetta Bertoldi called "Do Dead People Watch You Shower." I was thrilled to learn that they continue to lead their lives but can be with us to comfort us whenever we need them.

My journey of discovery has had an unpredictable outcome. Not only am I no longer fearful of death, I have gone from disbelief to hope and faith to a one hundred percent knowing that we survive physical death. I am the author of a best-selling book called We Don't Die - A Skeptic's Discovery of Life After Death and host of a global podcast called We Don't Die Radio. I am in the spirit world's hands, and have signed up for whatever they need me to do for humanity. They have given me the best friends of my life and the best adventures I could never have imagined.

Sandra M. Champlain

The fear of dying led Sandra Champlain on a 15-year journey to find evidence of the afterlife. She privately studied the worlds of psychic ability, mediumship, past life regression, near-death experiences, induced after death communication, reincarnation, electronic voice phenomena, dowsing, and remote viewing. Her fears were rested when she determined that there is sufficient proof that we don't die. After the death of her father, she created "How to Survive Grief," a free audio that was quickly heard by thousands worldwide. Armed with this powerful information that has reduced pain and saved lives, she wrote the international bestseller, "We Don't Die - A Skeptic's Discovery of Life After Death." Sandra is a highly respected speaker, author, entrepreneur and subject of the documentary by Emmy-award winning Robert Lyon, "We Don't Die - Documenting A Skeptic's Discovery of Life After Death." She hosts two radio programs "We Don't Die Radio" with now more than 350 episodes and "Shades of the Afterlife" on iHeartRadio. Find out more at www.sandrachamplain.com

Dear Reader,

I purposely choose to end this book with Sandra's story, because I so admire her strengths and positivity, and what she is doing for the world. The Fear of Death scenario she developed was very real and she could have let it become her story, but instead she dove deeply into the study of it and all other spiritual phenomena. Through her research, and acquainting herself with people who survived the experience of dying and coming back through her podcast interviews, she questioned everything with a skeptic's circumspection, until her fears no longer defined her, and a knowing of what comes after this life took its place.

I recognize her quest for knowledge in this arena, and applaud her tenacity to want to know more, as I also share that mantra. I thank her for being a strong book-end to these stories, and have hope that you will continue to feed your own spark my friends, and push to know more about the wonders of the After-Life, and your personal journey within the Light.

Written with Love for You,

Claudia Watts Edge

WITH GRATITUDE

To the wonderful souls who contributed their personal stories to this collection, and have now become new friends.

I wish to give thanks to those around me who allowed me to climb deeply into myself as I went through this book birthing. It is a labor of love that takes me over, while eating or even getting dressed is an earthly bother, especially in the last weeks of this process.

To my husband Chris, whose computer skills completely outweigh mine, and saved many a hair pulling session as he stepped in to save my work and calm me down. I am forever grateful for his love and tolerance of the evolving me that grows ever stronger in this work of the light.

Thank you to my wonderful children Sarah, Jesse, Aaron, Eric, and Chelsea Rose who have supported me in ways they don't even know, and whom I love with all of my heart.

To my sweet grandbabies who are a constant source of lessons, from patience and tolerance to letting go of worries and laughing with child-like abandon. The magical number of twelve little wonders, Andrew, Ava, Jude, Addison, Zoe, Jaydan, Harper, Violet, Sawyer, Churchill, Jessica and Joey give me purpose to rise and shine, and appreciate every single day.

To my friends, family, followers, and readers of my books who have offered your support throughout my journey, I thank you for the kind words and back slapping atta-girl assessments of my work. It has meant more than you will ever know.

My sincere thanks to Dr. Raymond Moody for the kind review of the book, my heart still skips a beat to know this man whom has documented thousands of cases over 50 years of research found my work worthy of a nod, I am twitterpated!

Thank you to Rev. Dr. Lee Witting of IANDS Radio for the contribution of your amazing personal story, review, and for putting me on your NDE program 8/3/2020.

A special shout out to Reverend Bill McDonald Jr. who came in this project with a sincere intent to help with all that I might need, even while going through his own personal health issues, a true friend and spiritual warrior indeed.

And last but not least to Dear Lilia, who came into my life with such a full heart and aimed the power of her unconditional love directly at me. I cannot thank her enough for all she has done for both the book and for me personally. A divinely guided friend that lifts me from what I thought I could do, into so much more than I ever imagined.

With love and gratitude for you all,

Claudia Watts Edge